Little Lionheart

Jana Bontrager

Copyright © 2015 Jana Bontrager
ISBN-13: 978-1507596586
ISBN-10: 1507596588

All rights reserved. No part of this book may be used for reproduced in any manner whatsoever without written permission. For information address Jana Bontrager.

Printed in the United States.
Printed and distributed by CreateSpace.

If you purchase this book without a cover, you should be aware that this book is stolen property. It was reported as "unsold or destroyed" to the publisher, and neither the author nor the publisher has received any payment for this "stripped book."

Property of
Piedmont Park
Alliance Church

A gift from our friend, Tara Teuscher. It hangs in our bedroom.

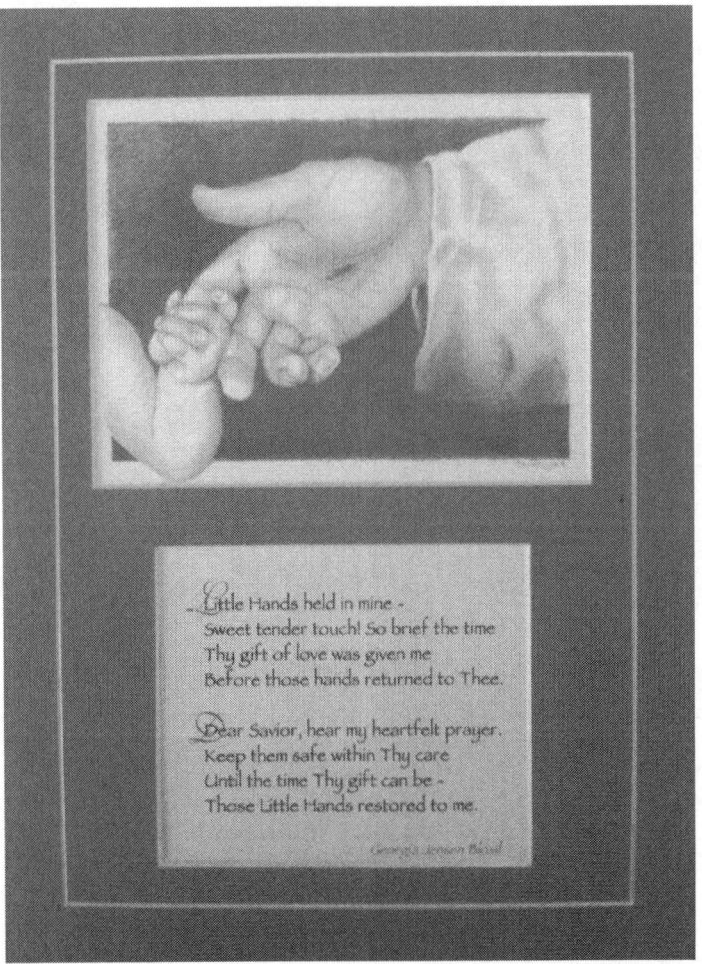

LITTLE LIONHEART

Dedicated to my loving husband.

Introduction

My family is a mixed one. I am married to my second husband Scott. I am Scott's third wife. As you may have guessed, this means that our children are kind of a mixed bag, but they are all ours nonetheless. In his first marriage, Scott had two children. Mary, our oldest, is an adult living on her own in Idaho, and Benjamin is a thriving teenager still living with us. In my first marriage, I gave birth to a daughter, Jolene, who we affectionately call JoJo. She is presently living with her father in Florida. Scott and I have a daughter, Sara, who is three years younger than JoJo. After Sara was born, Scott and I were content with our four children, but God had different plans. Christopher came.

The layout of this book is somewhat unorthodox for a novel, and as an English teacher, I feel the need to clarify how and why I've formatted *Little Lionheart* this way. The first words written in the first chapter of this book were not intended to be a book at all. I started a blog about Christopher and his condition when we discovered his heart defect on the twenty-week ultrasound during my pregnancy. The blog served as a means of mass communication.

You see, my family has lived all over the country. No, we are not a military family. We've just relocated over thousands of miles a few times. Up to this point, all of our children and myself were born in the Panhandle of Florida. Scott was born in New Orleans. At six months old, his family moved to our hometown in Florida. Not Disney-World-and-beaches Florida. Little-backwoods-one-horse-town-with-two-stop-lights Florida. Blountstown. The Deep South. At thirty-two and twenty-three respectively, Scott and I left our lifetime home and moved to the big, wide West in Idaho. For five years, we lived happily in Idaho until an event made us realize how far from "home" we were.

Scott's sister, Gladys, was living with a heart transplant and had been for seventeen years. When she passed away, we, of course, were going to her funeral in New Orleans where she lived. New Orleans, Louisiana is 1,870 miles from Pocatello, Idaho. Flying was too expensive for all of us on such short notice, so we drove. It was a hard trip on our family in so many ways. Emotionally, physically, financially and logistically.

After Gladys passed away, we knew we needed to be closer to our extended family. Within a day's drive at least. In Idaho we were over a thousand miles from our nearest relative. Although we absolutely loved Idaho, we decided it was just too far away, so we moved back East. Scott found a good job in Kingsport, Tennessee. We've been here for a couple of years now, and the time we've spent in the Blue Ridge Mountains of East Tennessee is where this journey takes place.

That's why I created the blog. Our family and friends in Florida, Idaho and Tennessee—as well as family scattered all over the US—wanted to know what was happening with our Christopher. We wanted them to know. Mass texts and phone trees didn't seem realistic to communicate with upwards of a thousand people who wanted to be informed of our baby's journey, so a nurse at the prestigious Monroe Carell Jr. Children's Hospital at Vanderbilt University suggested a blog. I've wanted to become a writer for a long time, and so I wrote. Now I'm using my blog to share Christopher's story with you. You'll see my blog entries throughout this book. I've used them as a timeline for what I shared with others in real time. The sections following the blog entries provide a broader scope and a more raw reality of our journey.

Friday, January 4, 2013

Overview of Christopher's Condition

Since there are so many people around the country who we want to keep informed about the news of Christopher, a nurse at Vanderbilt suggested we start a blog to keep everyone informed without posting on Facebook or calling/texting everyone we know. We want to sincerely thank all of you who have sent up prayers already on Christopher's behalf. We strongly believe in the power of prayer, and we are trusting that Christopher's condition is completely in God's hands.

A basic overview of his condition is that he has been diagnosed with hypoplastic left heart syndrome (HLHS). What this means is that the left side of his heart has not developed correctly and, as per the doctors' prediction, will never function. We need both sides of our hearts to get blood to and from the body and lungs, of course. Treatment to fix it to where Christopher's heart will get the job done with only the right side of his heart working will require three surgeries: 1) within his first week of life he will have the first surgery and his recovery time will be a minimum of four weeks in the NICU (Neonatal Intensive Care Unit), after which his immune system will be fragile and extra precautions will need to be taken even after he comes home until his second surgery, 2) at 4-6 months a second surgery will take place and after this surgery his fragile state and the risk factors get much better and he can resume life like a normal baby, 3) the last surgery will take place when he is between 2 and 3 years old, again with the risk factor being very low. Our biggest concerns are the first surgery and his recovery and health before the second surgery. Unfortunately we won't be able to have many visitors at once and certainly no one around him who is sick. Even taking him to the grocery store or to church will not be possible so as not to expose him to anything unnecessarily.

There is no need to worry about his condition as long as he is in the womb. His heart has natural modifications that allow his heart to be aided by mine. As long as I am pregnant with him, he is safe.

The doctors have assured us that, assuming all the treatment goes well, Christopher will be very much like every other perfectly healthy child. His only limitation will be that he won't have much endurance for long-distance running and other things like that (of course, neither do I and I have both sides of my heart working perfectly). So we are very thankful that this condition has the potential to be fixed.

Our other kids are doing very well and all seem to understand (as well as they can) about their baby brother's condition and treatment. They are all very excited to see him. Mary has plans to be at Vanderbilt with us when Christopher is born, and Benjamin and Sara will both be there for about a week when he is born. Of course, Benjamin will need to come back to school before too long.

Scott and I are doing well wrapping our heads around what's happening and what needs to be done. We are unsure how long Scott will be staying in Nashville, but he will have to come back to Kingsport at some point before Christopher is discharged for work and to be home with Benjamin. I will be living in Nashville for the duration of Christopher's stay. The hospital has been very helpful in assuring us that they will help us find accommodations and such. We have several contacts of people living in the Nashville area who are willing to help us out if need be, and we are very grateful for that support.

My future postings will be more brief as we update everyone on what is happening. Again, I would like to thank everyone who has had us in their thoughts and prayers thus far. It has been so very comforting to know that so many are concerned about all of us and our new little one. Questions are perfectly welcome. May God bless you all!

Due Date

I forgot to post the date Christopher is scheduled to be born. His birthday will be February 25th, 2013.

We knew the exact date Christopher would be born because he was to be born via C-section. JoJo and Sara were both born C-sections because of my complications during labor with JoJo. Both of the girls were born this way without a hitch, so if it ain't broke, don't change it during a high-risk pregnancy.

The tone of this blog post was upbeat and encouraging. Inside of us, though, was a storm of fear and anxiety. I saw no need to paint any more of a fearful picture than what this information already possessed. I saw it as my job not to throw a pity-party but to be strong and stoic for those who felt powerless to help. That was the sentiment from most people who were involved. They wanted to help, but there was nothing they could do.

Scott and I felt helpless and vulnerable at first, but we weren't. We *could* do something. We could remain calm for our other children and help them to find strength in us. We could seek the best care possible for our baby boy. We could plan for the complicated lifestyle we were in for. I could keep myself healthy and by proxy give Christopher the best possible chance to live with his challenge. And we could pray. God knows we prayed! I'm sure sometimes the Good Lord was the only one who could understand some of the prayers I sent up because at times they were just utterings and gurgles through the tears. But He heard. He responded with comfort and strength. My humanly self could not have possibly gotten through those final months of pregnancy without Devine Comfort.

I prayed for all sorts of scenarios. I prayed for Christopher to be miraculously healed. I prayed that all the testing that showed is heart defect was wrong. I prayed that something be wrong with me instead of him. But the prayer that I was led to pray by the deepest stirrings of my soul was, "God, let

Your Will be done. Help me to accept what Your Plan is." Boy, that was hard to swallow! What my imperfect instincts said was, "God, just let Christopher be okay no matter what, because that's what I want. Just fix it. Period." But I prayed for His Will to be done.

Tuesday, January 8, 2013

Local Cardiologist Visit

The visit to the local cardiologist today revealed no new news. However, I did learn how closely the cardiologist here in Kingsport will be working with the team of doctors in Vanderbilt. The local cardiologist (who will be Christopher's cardio doc when he comes home from Vandy) has been communicating with Vanderbilt through all of our visits and will be following Christopher's progress throughout the whole surgery/recovery process. This was a relief to me to have someone so close to home to be working on Christopher's case. We continue to be impressed, relieved and thankful that Vanderbilt's doctors, nurses and staff have everything so well organized. Christopher is in good hands.

On a much lighter note, Christopher remains very active which reassures us that he is doing well and growing healthy. Sometimes it even feels like he has the hiccups. Ultrasound measurements show that his growth is perfectly normal. All of his other organs look wonderfully normal.

These check-ups were stressful. Scott came with me to as many as he could. Each time we waited with bated breath at what else could possibly be wrong. We were told with HLHS kids it isn't uncommon for them to have other organs which give them trouble besides the heart. Kidneys, lungs, brain, pretty much anything else could be compromised. That's why the checklist of healthy organs was such a relief. He would only have to deal with half of a heart. Only. What an understatement!

During this time between doctors' visits, we were preparing for the storm. We stored away money like a squirrel stores nuts for the winter. I was working as a middle school English teacher at the time, but after our baby boy was born, he would need round-the-clock care, so my income would go away. We would not be impoverished by this economic change, but it would hurt us financially, especially with all of the extra expense of a special needs child.

Scott had an excellent job as a Physician Assistant. It was a comfort having someone with a medical background near. He worked in a family practice as a healthcare provider and was extremely good at his job. He watched my health closely for my sake and for Christopher's, and he served as my translator for doctors' visits. It was wonderful for me, but as I discovered after a while, not so much for him.

Scott could foresee—but wisely did not share with me—all of the possible physical repercussions of Christopher's condition. His mind reeled at the avenues that our son might have to travel. It would have driven me crazy. The information I *had* was scaring the life out of me! But Scott kept trudging forward doing what he does best: taking care of our family.

Friday, January 11, 2013

Weekly OB Visits

As a precaution, I have been monitored by my local OB doctor on a weekly basis for about a month. These weekly appointments will continue until the time that Christopher is delivered. The reason for the frequent visits is mainly to ensure that no early labor will happen. The plan for delivery is to be at Vanderbilt when Christopher is born. Delivering him away from Vanderbilt would require emergency transportation to Vandy, which can be arranged, but would not be the best-case-scenario. Yesterday was my latest appointment and everything looks to be right on schedule.

We are looking into living arrangements for the long-term stay in Nashville and have been given some good options. The Ronald McDonald House is one option that seems to be a good fit, but we have not made a solid plan.

My parents and Scott's mom are planning to be there with us when Christopher is born. I can't help but feel that God brought us back to the Southeast just in time to be close enough for travel to be possible for our family.

Both Benjamin and Sara have expressed interest in Christopher sharing a room with them when he comes home (I think Benjamin has changed his mind), but it is so sweet that they both even offered the option of sharing their room with their new brother. Sara has told me on several occasions, "Mama, you don't have to do anything to take care of Christopher. I will take care of him all the time."

Since I was trying to work as much as possible at the time, I didn't want to take off work to go to the OB checkups once a week. I had no sick leave because I was a full-time substitute, not a contracted teacher. Time off meant money off, and with the impending out-of-work situation, we just couldn't afford it. So one afternoon every week I left the school—even beating the busses leaving the building—and went straight to Dr. Saunders's office for a weight, blood pressure and ultrasound check. Each visit was like holding my breath from the moment I walked through the office door until the time the checks were completed and was told things were progressing normally.

As I mentioned in my first blog entry, Christopher was completely safe and his heart function did not impact his survival in the womb. As long as he was with me, he was safe. I've never had such conflicting emotions before. Part of me was so very happy to meet my son. The other part was terrified for him to leave the security of my body. I cried in fear almost every day at some point. I wanted so badly for something to be wrong with me instead.

When I was pregnant with Sara, I was finalizing my divorce from my first husband. Due to the tremendous stress of the situation, my blood pressure skyrocketed. At one point it was clocked at 181/162. If you're not familiar with blood pressure numbers, 120/80 is normal. The nurse who took my blood pressure for that elevated reading gaped at the gauge. The doctor told me I was in "stroke range." I was medicated and at the end of the pregnancy put on bed rest. Through that whole ordeal, I was never truly frightened. Concerned, yes. But never scared. I had faith in my body's ability to endure whatever I needed to keep my daughter safe. That's why I wanted something to be wrong with me instead of Christopher. I am a relatively healthy adult, but he was so little. A baby's health is precarious anyway even when there isn't anatomic anomaly. I couldn't handle the thought that I could not take this defect away from him somehow and take it on myself. I was powerless once he left my body. I told myself that I could handle being pregnant forever. Of course, that wasn't possible.

Thursday, January 17, 2013

5 1/2 Weeks to Go!

Yesterday was my weekly OB visit, and everything looks great. No early labor and Christopher is growing right on schedule. His heart rate is strong! I'm on a first name basis with the ultrasound techs and nurses.

Monday, January 28, 2013

Four Weeks from Today

Today marks four weeks until Christopher is to be born! I knew that time would fly after Christmas, but I still can't believe how close it's getting. It has been fun preparing for his arrival. Sara is stoked about sharing her room and asks every day when we are going to put Christopher's crib together and set it up in her bedroom. I'm excited to see it all set up, too. The theme for his bedding is *The Lion King* because Scott has said that he already has "the heart of a lion."

My latest OB visit revealed no new news. The latest ultrasound caught him practicing breathing! I am feeling wonderful. I keep saying that I don't know how much farther my body can stretch, but Scott says I've been saying that for two months now. I'm glad for the expansion because that means Christopher is growing. He is kicking less now and rolling more. Ultrasound images show that he is getting pretty crowded, so the room he had to kick is running out!

Our church gave us a baby shower two Sundays ago, and we received lots of wonderful gifts that will make our preparation for Christopher's arrival very easy. We feel very blessed to have found such a wonderful church family!

Being five hours from our nearest relative was difficult during this stressful time. Our church family at Southview Community Church of the Nazarene was our surrogate family. Those people looked after all of us from day one. When we moved to Kingsport, we knew we wanted to be involved in a church, so we went "church shopping." Southview was the first church we visited, and we saw no need to go anywhere else. We had found where we fit.

It was a small church, but we liked that part of it. Our pastor, Tom Legg, was the first person in the church who we told about Christopher's heart condition. We kind of blurted it out after a service one Wednesday night. Someone else could easily have heard, but we were so desperate for prayer and to unburden ourselves from the secrecy that we sat on the front row chairs and cried as we told him, and he prayed with us. It didn't take long for the prayer chain to begin.

In the previous few years, two other families in this small congregation had children born with special needs. The Rudes were the most recent.

Their son Coen, who was a year old at the time, was born with a cleft palette and some skeletal muscular challenges. He was doing well, but he was going to face some difficult developmental hurtles in his young life.

The Coens (coincidently, their last name is the same as Coen Rude's first name) had a daughter named Sydnee who had a laundry list of special needs including cancer. Despite her challenges, Sydnee was a vibrant little girl. She endured 15 surgeries in her four years of life including having both legs amputated below the knees and still always had a smile on her face. Sydnee died on August 30, 2010. We moved to Kingsport after her death, so we never met her. I feel like I know her because of how people describe her. Full of life. Tough. Sweet as sugar. Never let her challenges define her. I wanted that for my son. I wanted him to thrive despite what he faced. My heart ached for the Coens. They were so strong and unified after losing a child. I didn't know how they did it. And I hoped I would never have to find out.

Monday, February 4, 2013

Countdown: 21 Days!

Yes, time is flying! Three weeks from today we will meet the newest member of our family face-to-face. Our excitement and joy far outweigh our fear at this point. We have faith that God may grant miraculous healing of Christopher's heart, but if that is not in His Will, we believe that He has led us to the best course of action to get our new little one the best care possible. Either way, God's hand is in this situation.

Some people have asked about whether I've been able to continue working until delivery. Barring any complications, I will be able to work right up until the Friday (Feb. 22nd) before Christopher is born on the following Monday (Feb. 25th). I am very thankful for this for two reasons: 1) it helps financially and 2) it has provided a haven for me during the time that I was wrapping my head around the situation. My latest OB visit last Thursday showed that everything is still right on schedule.

Scott and I are heading to Vanderbilt for our final visit before the *big* visit. We will be meeting with the high-risk OB and the cardiologist who will perform Christopher's surgeries. Also during this visit we will be touring the NICU which I'm excited about. Seeing the actual environment where Christopher will be kept will put several anxieties to rest and answer lots of questions like "How much access will we actually have to him while he is in recovery?"

The crib has been put together, diapers are being stock-piled and our home is teeming with the excitement of our new little one entering the world!

Can you feel the positive energy? If you can, I faked it well. We *were* excited, but along with excitement was anxiety and fear. I felt like a vice was tightening around my heart as each day passed. I cried almost every day on my drive home from work because the tears that I had been holding back all during work couldn't be held back anymore. It sounds like a terrible time, and in some ways it was, but there was joy, too.

I found mine mainly in my other kids. Their excitement for their new baby brother was contagious. Benjamin is the best big brother any kid could ask for, and he was so stoked about having another boy in the house he could hardly stand it. Sara is a born nurturer, so she was happy to have a living thing she could take care of, and a little brother would be just the thing for her little maternal instincts.

Christopher's other sisters were not living with us, but Mary and JoJo were excited, too. When Mary lived with us, she and Sara were as close as two sisters could be. The fourteen years of age difference between those two melts away to nothing when they watch movies together or ride horses, so we knew that a new baby brother would be loved more than he could stand by Mary.

The last time I saw Jolene with a baby was when Sara was that little. JoJo was two-and-a-half at that time, so I wasn't sure how comfortable she would be around an infant. Especially one in the fragile state that Christopher was to be. I knew how mature and intelligent she was for her age, though, so I wasn't worried.

Saturday, February 9, 2013

Vanderbilt Visit Before THE Visit...

Scott and I went to our last appointments at Vanderbilt Children's Hospital before we go for Christopher's delivery. Everything checked out just fine (as fine as it can be with his condition) and we even found out that Christopher already weighs around 6 and 1/2 pounds! Like every other visit, we saw just how "together" the doctors, nurses, and staff at Vanderbilt have things organized. They leave nothing up to chance and are excellent at communicating. We really feel blessed to have Christopher being taken care of by such a wonderful place.

Our tour of the NICU was what we were the most excited/curious to see on this visit. I was afraid that we would have very little access to Christopher while he is in the NICU, but it turns out that this is not the case at all. In fact, everyone who will be with us at delivery (all of our parents, and even Sara) will be able to go spend time with him while he is in the incubator. We probably won't be able to hold him much because of IVs and such, but the NICU representative who gave us the tour said that they encourage people to touch him as much as possible. "Since physical touch is very important to newborns, it will actually help him to deal with things better," she said.

The schedule of travel and delivery is still the same. We will go to Nashville on Sunday the 24th and delivery will be the morning of the 25th.

Christopher's Story

I have been feeling very good these past few weeks. The only issue is that I keep knocking things off of tables and counters with my ever-expanding tummy! Scott, Benjamin and Sara are all doing well. Life is pretty normal around our house right now, but the anticipation of what is to come looms in all of us.

I've mentioned this before, but I can't stop being grateful for all of the wonderful people who are thinking of us and praying for us. The outpour of concern has been more than we could ever imagine. I cannot express enough how big of a comfort our friends and family have been. I have to chalk up our strength through all of this to the support of our loved ones and God Himself. Without these things, this would be more than we could handle. As it is, we are ready to face this challenge head-on with confidence that everything will be okay.

Living in Florida from birth until young adulthood, I witnessed my fair share of hurricanes come ashore. I liken the feeling of awaiting Christopher's arrival to preparing for a huge hurricane. The news says a whopper of a storm is coming. You can see the cyclone on the vast blue Gulf of Mexico on the green screen map on television. The local news stations used to distribute blank maps of the Gulf Coast and Gulf of Mexico—before the internet was so common—through newspapers and convenience stores so that people could watch the weather report and chart a storm's progress. The pediatric cardio specialist at Vandy drew us a "map" of what Christopher's heart looked like as opposed to a normal heart. The left side looked shriveled up and solid instead of plump and cavernous the way it was supposed to. I won't get too specific about the ins and outs of the surgical corrections she showed us—largely because it makes my head spin—but she walked us through how Christopher's heart would function providing all of the corrective surgeries did what they should. It was a map of survival for him.

Tales of storms of old are recounted as a fresh hurricane approaches. Around my childhood home it was the tale of hurricane Opal in 1995 that I remember most. I remember it because Opal was the storm that demolished our old beach cottage on Mexico Beach. I sought out stories of babies with Christopher's condition, not to frighten myself, but to help me to know what we were facing. I did not feel that ignorance was bliss. The more I knew, the better. A distant cousin of mine named Miranda whom I hadn't connected with in years shared her son Kellen's story of his congenital heart defect. Although it was not the same condition that my son had, I was reaching for anything I could find. At Miranda's suggestion I joined a Facebook group called Heart Mamas. Here there were all kinds of stories. I forced myself to focus on the good ones although it was impossible to completely ignore the ones that ended in tragedy. So many of them did. But I had faith that my son's story would be triumphant.

Emergency preparedness supplies are purchased for any category of hurricane. Everyone gets ready to "batten down the hatches." Materially preparing for any new baby takes thought and effort. Preparing for a special needs baby is the difference between preparing for a tropical storm versus a category five storm. Along with diapers, wipes and bottles, we had to think of a movement-sensored baby monitor that alarms if the baby stops breathing. We needed to brush up on infant CPR and have a specific emergency plan in place. We ordered special high-calorie formula—to add to my breast milk—to keep up with Christopher's caloric demands of a new baby whose heart was working overtime to make up for the two missing chambers. And a hundred other details that we would learn about as we went.

You look up at the sky, and it is clear and blue. For all you can see around you, you'd think it is just another hot August day. The danger cannot be seen, felt or heard, but you know it is coming. I felt great in my pregnancy. Christopher kicked regularly—sometimes very hard—and had the hiccups several times a day. Had it not been for modern medicine, we would have no idea based on my gestational physiology that anything was wrong.

Friday, February 15, 2013

Ten Days and Counting...

The latest OB visits have been good news. No signs of early labor, and although they toyed with the possibility of putting me on bed rest for next week, Dr. Saunders assured me that working until next Friday is safe for me and Christopher. I will be going for two check-ups next week, so they are keeping a very close eye on the situation.

I keep thinking how strange it will be to be recovering from childbirth without a little one to take care of in the middle of the night or diapers to change or baths to give or clothes to change or burping to do. I have a friend at church named Kristi Coen who has been a nurse in the NICU and she has assured me that our involvement will be encouraged as much as possible while Christopher is under the NICU's care. She said that things like cuddling and talking to him have shown to improve a baby's recovery and growth in these situations. I sure hope so.

I keep saying "thank you" for all the positive words and prayers from everyone, but "thank you" doesn't begin to describe how much it means to have so many people who are so dear to us to be with us during this time (even from afar). I get overwhelmed at the generosity and encouragement from our friends and family. It is uplifting to know that we are not alone during this complicated situation. Thank God and thank you for being there for us!

In my imagination I had some sort of sci-fi scenario concocted for intensive care. I had never been in any intensive care unit before, let alone one for infants. I imagined large incubators with plastic glove holes on the walls for clear-coated access to my son. Nurses and doctors in HazMat suits. Everything white and sterile and hostile. I wanted to be with my baby and along with all of the other warranted fears, I was creating some in my own imagination.

Tuesday, February 19, 2013

Packed and Ready

Dr. Saunders is keeping a watchful eye on things. I had a check-up yesterday, I have one tomorrow, and I won't be surprised if he has me come back on Friday. Whew! I'm still working, and my classroom neighbors, Maureen and Robin, keep looking in on me to make sure things are okay.

When people walk up to me now, their eyes don't meet mine. Their gaze automatically drifts to my ever expanding tummy. I find it comical. I even had a complete stranger walk up to me in Walmart and touch my belly. I have to say that I don't think I'll ever get used to that, but some people just can't help themselves.

We are getting bags packed just in case (Heaven forbid) we need to go to Nashville before

Sunday. I will post short updates more frequently now just to let you know that all's well.

"I'm on pins and needles." Whoever coined that phrase must have been waiting for a special needs baby to be born. I was so conflicted during this time. I wanted to meet Christopher, but I wanted to keep him safe just like he was.

Wednesday, February 20, 2013

Time to Go to Nashville

Today Dr. Saunders said we should go to Nashville soon. Because of Christopher's shift to the birth canal and my feeling different over the past two days, Dr. Saunders wanted to air on the side of caution and have us go to Nashville early to avoid going into labor here in Kingsport.

Scott and I will go on to Nashville in the morning. Some very good friends of ours from our church have been gracious enough to take care of Benjamin and Sara while we spend these next few days in Nashville. Thank you so much to John and Melinda Hale for being willing to do this for us! Without their generosity both kids would be stuck sitting in a room with us as I am supposed to be on bed rest and Scott does not want to leave me. Since Melinda and John were planning to come be with us at Vanderbilt when Christopher is born, they will bring Benjamin and Sara with them when they come on Sunday.

Mom, Dad and Annette are on standby. Delivery is still scheduled for Monday, so hopefully their plans won't have to change. Going over early is just a precaution. Scott and I will both feel better once we get to Nashville. Stay tuned for the rest of the story...

My "nesting" instinct was driving me and Scott crazy. I did *not* want to stay still and off of my feet. Scott knew I needed to and scolded me when I got to stirring around. I can't blame him. He knew it was imperative that I rest. I wanted to waddle around the house making preparations for our premature departure, but he and the kids stepped up and took care of everything. I felt like a very lucky woman as I watched how diligently they worked.

The grandparents all live in the panhandle of Florida which is over seven hours from Nashville. Knowing them all the way I do, I can imagine all of them sitting like coiled springs ready to rush to Tennessee at the ring of a phone. I bet they got little to no sleep those last few days before they headed to Vanderbilt.

Friday, February 22, 2013

<u>Hurry Up and Wait</u>

We made it to Nashville last night. We were even able to get a checkup from one of the doctors at Vandy because they wanted to make sure everything was still going well. So now, we wait. We are here and that's where we should be. Our anxiety level has dropped significantly being this close to the hospital and Christopher's doctors. Had I delivered in Kingsport, he would have had to be taken by helicopter to Nashville. That would *not* have made me happy. As it is, God has put us right where we need to be.

Benjamin and Sara are doing well staying with our friends from church.

Scott and I were able to get a short-term apartment with the Walmart Hospitality House. (I take back every bad thing I've ever said about Walmart.) Not only is it convenient to the hospital and affordable, but it is going to be a very comfortable place for us to stay while we are so far from home.

Prayers are being answered. God is working in this. That is the biggest comfort of all.

Living arrangements for our time in Nashville were a concern. We knew we would probably be there for over a month, so a hotel—even a very cheap one—would be more than we could afford. The hospital helped us to make arrangements, but those arrangements could not be solidified until we got to Nashville for the stay. Our options ranged from The Ronald McDonald House to Extended Stay America hotel. All of the possibilities were good ones, but not knowing exactly where we would be worried me. I like to have things like this planned ahead of time.

The Walmart Hospitality House was by far our most desirable option. It was an actual apartment with a full kitchen, living room and bedrooms. The Ronald McDonald House would have been great too, but things like the living area and kitchen were common areas in the building. Since we would have quite a few people staying, the apartment fit best. As we exited the interstate and headed for the hospital, a patient relations representative from Vandy called us to tell us we would have the apartment for as long as we needed it.

Saturday, February 23, 2013

Still Waiting...

All is well. I'm feeling tired today but not having this baby yet.

"Tired" is an understatement. I was feeling drained. The night before, Scott and I had overdone it for my condition. We watch a show on the Food Network called *Diners, Drive-Ins and Dives* with host Guy Fieri, and *Triple D*—as it is called—has featured numerous restaurants in Nashville, one of which was right around the corner from where we were staying in the Hospitality House apartments. We couldn't resist eating there, and I was feeling very good even after the four hour drive the day before. So we went and enjoyed some Cajun cooking that was delectable! That evening we also visited one of the malls in Nashville and, of course, walked quite a bit. We also saw a movie. Needless to say, it was a busy evening which I paid for the next day with exhaustion.

Sunday, February 24, 2013

The Eve of Christopher

I've been resting *all day*! I feel very good, and we are ready to meet our new baby boy tomorrow. He is scheduled for delivery at 8:30 unless, of course, someone else comes in with an emergency.

My parents and Scott's mom have all made it safely to Nashville and the kids will be here soon. All is well. My next blog should be tomorrow to announce Christopher's arrival!

The main reason Dr. Saunders in Kingsport wanted us to come to Nashville a few days early was because I said I was "feeling funny." Since I had never truly been in labor—even the early stages—I didn't know what any type of labor symptoms were. I had experienced the beginnings of contractions before the emergency C-section with Jolene because the labor was induced in the hospital, but that had been seven years prior to this. I was still feeling funny and chalked it up to my being so tired. While sitting on the futon in the living room watching television I was feeling the normal kicks of Christopher. Then I felt a different type of movement. It was like he was stretching out in all directions. My belly tensed and seemed to expand. It only lasted for ten seconds or so. It never crossed my mind that I might be in labor because my two girls seemed to be in no hurry to be born. But Christopher was different. The "kicking everywhere at once" happened a few more times, but there was absolutely no pain and nothing else happened, so we went to bed.

Scott and I got our last night's sleep before our lives were changed forever. Having a baby always changes the dynamics of a family, but Christopher would be a force like no other.

Monday, February 25, 2013

He is Here!!!

Christopher Scott Bontrager was born today at 9:11 am, weighed 7 pounds 10 ounces and was 21 inches long. The delivery went off without a hitch and the little man was pink and crying the second he emerged into this world. After a quick clean-up and brief intro to mom and dad, he was whisked to the NICU. There he was evaluated and prepped with the meds he will need before his first operation.

A few speed bumps were laid out for him as they tried to get IVs placed, but we were assured by two different doctors that he is doing well in spite of this. He also has a bit of an issue with breathing and might need a tube to assist him, but that hasn't happened yet. All in all we have been told that they are very satisfied with his condition so far.

The estimated date of his surgery is Thursday. That is subject to change, but it is a time to work with.

I haven't seen him much today, but I did get to venture this evening to his bedside to caress and talk to him. I even got to change his diaper. Scott has been in and out of the NICU all day. He is absolutely beautiful! He has a head full of black hair and big, dark eyes. I can't wait to see him tomorrow!

When we arrived at the hospital the morning of Christopher's birth, we checked in and did all the things I expected for a planned C-section delivery. We chatted with our nurse who was very sweet and competent. I would expect nothing less from Vanderbilt. She told us that her daughter was an actress. When we asked if we might have seen her in something, she asked, "Have you seen the show *Pretty Little Liars*?"

"I've never seen it, but I've seen commericals," I replied expecting that her daughter had been perhaps a small character in an episode or two.

"Well, she's Lucy Hale who plays Aria Montgomery," she said as she pulled up a picture on her phone to show us.

I recognized her immediately! How cool to have a real celebrity's mother be my nurse! She then went on to tell us that Reese Witherspoon's mother used to work in Vanderbilt Hospital as well. I've never lived in a big city where famous people actually lived too, so I was a bit starstruck, which was nice for the moment. It took my mind off of my fears even if for a minute.

Then Lucy Hale's mother said, "I'm going to strap this monitor to your tummy so we can keep a watch on the little guy's vitals until they are ready for you in the OR." After she did so, she studied the bedside monitors for a moment. "How are you feeling?" she asked without taking her eyes from the screens.

"Fine," I replied with my usual Southern answer.

"Really..." it was more a statement than a question. "Because you're having contractions two minutes apart." Then she turned and looked at me with raised eyebrows.

"I am?" I asked leaving my mouth dropped open in disbelief.

Scott looked at me wide-eyed, and I could tell that he had just about entered panic mode. "I'm glad I didn't know that *before*!" I'm not sure if he was being sarcastic or not, but he was not happy with that piece of information.

"Well, you're in the right place, and things don't seem to be progressing too quickly, so we'll just keep an eye on things."

Then we waited for the operating room.

• • •

I had done the whole C-section thing twice before, so I was well-versed in what to expect. I knew the epidural would feel like a bee sting as they inserted the needle into my spine but then the pain would be done and I would just feel my lower body go numb. I knew that I would feel like I was going to be pulled off the table from all of the tugging the doctor would do as he opened my body to retrieve my child. I knew that it would feel like all of my insides were being scooped out when they pulled Christopher from the safety of my womb. I knew that Scott would rise from his place at my head to watch him being born over the sheet that they used to block my vision from the surgery. I knew that once my new baby was free of my body that I shouldn't panic if it took a few seconds before I heard his voice for the first time. Both Jolene and Sara had been a few seconds delayed with their first cry, so I expected Christopher to be as well.

The moment he left my body, Christopher sounded a loud, aggressive cry! I was shocked! They had told us to expect that he might struggle to breathe and might be born purple or even a dusky blue color, but he looked and sounded perfect! Tears ran from my eyes to my hair as I lay there still open from the birth. Scott kissed my forehead and said that he looked incredible!

There were a dozen people in the operating room on standby for anything that might be needed. It seemed like only a few seconds before Christopher was cleaned up and brought to where I still laid for his first kiss from his mother and father. I can't remember exactly what I whispered to him, but it was something like, "Be tough, little buddy." And then he was whisked away to begin the fight for his life.

Scott asked me weeks before where I would rather him be after Christopher was taken away in the operating room to begin IVs and medication. I told him without hesitation that he needed to go with our little boy. "Are you sure you don't want me to stay with you?" he had double checked.

"Absolutely not," was my firm answer. "I will be fine. I've been through this before, and he needs one of us to be with him."

It was torture to be away from my newborn. The nurses had me up and walking by 7:00 pm the day of delivery—which feels something like having your guts spilled out on the floor—but it meant that I could ride in a wheelchair to where Christopher was. Scott kept saying, "He's so handsome! He's such a good-looking kid!"

Tuesday, February 26, 2013

A Very Good Day...

After a few minor complications and adjustments to his care, our little boy is doing quite well! I got to hold him for the first time today for a precious few minutes, and the nurse said that his being held even for that short a time was worth hours of just being touched in the incubator. It was priceless!!!

The plan is for his first surgery to be on Thursday. His condition is stable, and he seems to be relatively comfortable considering all that he has dealt with over the first 36 hours of his life.

Prayers are constantly being said, heard and ANSWERED! This little guy is already a fighter, and we are excited to watch him come through this like a champion!

Scott was as big of a trooper as anyone. He spent his time running back and forth from me to Christopher. I could only go down to see Christopher for a little bit at a time, but I was grateful to see him all that I could. Holding him took me, Scott and the nurse to gather all of the wires that trailed from him. He looked so healthy, though. On the surface, it didn't make sense. Why couldn't we just take all of that stuff off of him and walk out of there? Underneath all the IVs and stickers and wires he looked perfect! But that was the danger, I guess. Had we not known, he would have looked fine, until he wasn't. We were in the right place doing the right things. I stayed as long as I could with him until I was falling asleep sitting up. It was hard to keep in perspective that I had been through surgery a day and a half before.

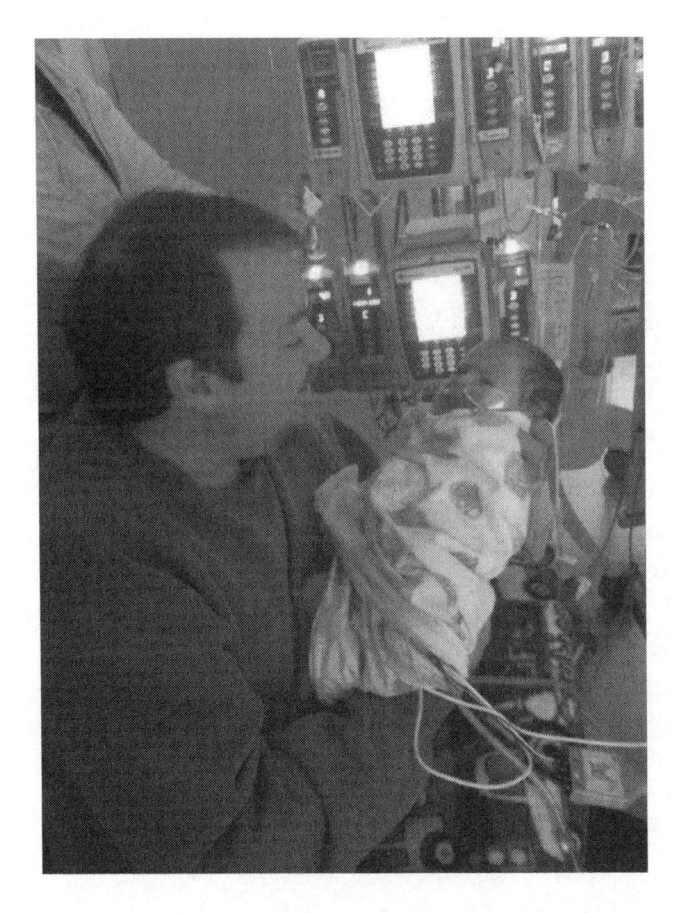

Scott's first time holding his youngest son.

Wednesday, February 27, 2013

The Eve of the First Surgery

Christopher continues to do well. We have spoken to numerous doctors about the procedure set for tomorrow at 8:30 am, and we have been assured that he has the best chances of coming through this well. He is a strong, healthy baby despite the heart condition, he has tolerated treatment well thus far, and all of his other organ systems are running perfectly normally. Make no mistake, we are still very nervous about our four-day-old going into the OR, but we feel much better knowing that the odds are in his favor.

I got discharged from the hospital today and am handling this C-section and recovery better than either of the other two. Maybe it's because Vanderbilt is a top-notch medical facility, or perhaps it's my will to be completely well so that we don't have something else to deal with. It's more likely that God has given me the gift of a quick recovery because He knows there are bigger issues to face.

Sara has had a bit of difficulty processing what she sees with Christopher. She is such a nurturing child that it upsets her to see her baby brother with the monitors and IVs. Benjamin has spent some quality time with Christopher, and Christopher has seemed to respond well to his "Bubba."

With an average baby with no complications one doesn't realize just how much human interaction affects a newborn. Normally a baby gets passed around and cuddled so much that the interaction is taken for granted. With Christopher I have seen just how stimulating a familiar voice can be for a baby. A caressing touch calms and soothes far more than I realized. The PICU (Pediatric Intensive Care Unit) nurses encourage family members (especially parents) to talk to and touch their incubated little one. Christopher's vital signs actually improve when one of us is interacting with him. He is calmed quickly upon becoming upset if Scott or me talks to him or strokes his arm. I am amazed at the effects of one human being to another.

Biggest, most risky surgery is tomorrow. Please keep praying. He hears you!!!

I prayed and prayed on this day. Every time the surgery crossed my mind, I prayed.

After I was discharged, I went straight up to the PICU to see Christopher. In intensive care only a few people were allowed into the unit per patient at one time. They are working constantly back there, so they don't need a crowd to deal with. Only three people were allowed in at once. When I got there, Sara, Scott and Benjamin were with Christopher. I waited in the hall for a minute outside of the locked doors to the unit, and then they all came out. The look on Sara's face made her feelings transparent. She was in agony for her baby brother.

"He looks so bad," she said.

"I know it is a lot, baby," I tried to comfort her.

Big tears had welled up in her brown eyes and dripped down her face, but she didn't make a sound. I had managed to kneel down to look eye-to-eye with her forgetting my own pain, but when she tried to climb up on my knee, I was reminded that, "Hey, you still have staples holding your gut shut!" I had to tell her I couldn't pick her up. I wanted to make her fear and sorrow go away, but I didn't know how other than to tell her that it would be okay.

• • •

The day of surgery Scott and I stood at Christopher's bedside as a team of nurses and surgical staff prepared to wheel him down to the operating room. I stood with my back to Scott and he pulled me to his chest with his arm around the front of me from one shoulder to the other. We both stood silently watching people come in and out. The head OR nurse came up to us. "Mom and Dad?" he asked. I can't remember the guy's name. I was a little stunned because he looked and sounded just like Justin Long, the actor. I hope my mouth wasn't open.

"Yes, I'm Scott and this is my wife Jana," Scott said as we both shook "Justin's" hand.

"I'll be the nurse in surgery today with Christopher. I've got both of your phone numbers to call and give you updates on his progress throughout surgery."

"That sounds great. How often will we hear from you?" I asked.

"I'll call about every 90 minutes or so, but don't freak out if it has been 91 minutes since I last updated you. It doesn't mean anything is wrong, sometimes it just isn't a good time to stop and call."

"Alright." I'm sure Scott and I both looked terrified.

"Everything will be fine. Christopher is healthy in every other way, and he seems to be strong. Now, Kristin will be here to be his nurse after Christopher returns to the PICU later this afternoon. She's the best."

"Aw, he's laying it on thick," the nurse with short hair and glasses said from behind the OR nurse. We had Kristin as Christopher's nurse the day before, but we hadn't gotten to know her very well, but the OR nurse's sincere confidence in her reassured us that our little boy would be well taken care of. "This guy here is the best in the business," Kristin said pointing to Justin Long's doppelganger. I could tell that the compliments were sincere and not just lip service for each other.

"We hope you both are as good as the other says," Scott interjected.

"We will all make sure that your little boy does well. He is in good hands. Dr. Bischelle is the best." The OR nurse told us we could ride down to the surgical floor and go to the waiting room from there. We followed the caravan of medical staff behind the rolling crib down the hall and onto the elevator.

In the oversized elevator my eyes were drawn upward. On the ceiling was a big, three-dimensional white goose against a blue, starry sky. I imagined older children riding in this elevator and finding a last minute's peace in the distraction of the beautiful figure before heading into surgery. Christopher, of course, couldn't tell what it was being as he was only four days old, but I like to think that maybe he liked the different colors.

We stepped out of the elevator. What we knew was about to happen seemed surreal. Scott and I kissed Christopher and watched him being wheeled down the hall. This surgery was the most dangerous. It was out of our hands.

Thursday, February 28, 2013

10:00am

He has been in surgery for about an hour. The nurse has called once to let us know that his vessels are handling the procedure well so far. I will post more as we hear it.

11:00 am

The OR nurse just called to tell us that everything is going as planned. They kept telling us that it was hard to tell how Christopher would handle surgery until they got into the OR with him. He is handling it well and there are no surprises. More to come as we hear.

1:00 pm

We have been notified that they are closing Christopher up and surgery went very well! They got finished far sooner than they expected! We are now waiting for the visit from the surgeon who will tell us that they are totally finished and how it went. Prayers ANSWERED!!!

The waiting room on the third floor of Vanderbilt Children's Hospital reminded me of an airport. We were a group of ten people waiting to hear about our little boy but there were upwards of a hundred others waiting as well. We watched as the lobby representative called to the families of patients and ushered them into the private rooms off of the large waiting area. We expected to have the news delivered to us the same way.

At about two o'clock a tall, thin man who appeared to be in his early sixties dressed in light blue scrubs and a surgical mask pulled down from his face around his neck locked eyes with me as he walked quickly across the full waiting room. He had a wide grin on his face and a bright look in his eyes. He reached for my husband's hand first as he said, "I've got great news about Christopher. The surgery could not have gone better! Christopher's anatomy allowed us to do a less dangerous procedure, and he came through it like a champ!"

We all heaved a collective sigh of relief! We listened as the doctor—who we realized by this time was Christopher's surgeon, Dr. Bischelle—tell us more details of the surgery. I tried to keep up, but I knew that what I didn't understand Scott would put in layman's terms for me later. All I needed to know at that point was that things had gone wonderfully! We all kept looking at each other saying, "'Couldn't have gone better!' Did you hear that?! 'Couldn't have gone better,' he said!"

Out of Surgery!!!

He is through surgery and it could not have gone better!!! His recovery is expected to be very smooth and much easier than it could have been. The doctor had nothing but positive things to say about the surgery and recovery. God is good and He had a hand on our baby boy.

Thank you with all my heart for your thoughts, prayers and encouragements!!!

That night, I felt more at peace than I had felt in months. The most dangerous of the surgeries which we were told only 80% of HLHS babies survive was done. Although we were nowhere near out of the woods yet, I felt that I could relax if only for that night. In my temporary euphoria, I was feeling grateful. So I wrote the following post:

Special Thanks

The nurses continue to make minor adjustments to Christopher to keep things like blood-pressure and heart rate stable. They are keeping him pretty sedated to keep him comfortable although I have caught him with his eyes open several times.

During this time of more relief than I could imagine I'd like to recognize and specifically thank some very special people. Our church family, specifically John and Melinda Hale, have been standing with us in faith and prayer all these months and have been selfless in offering love and support. Pastor Tom and his wife Lynn even drove over the day Christopher was born.

My mother-in-law Annette has not only come to be here while Christopher was born and underwent surgery, but she will be staying indefinitely to help with whatever we need. She is a big help and comfort. She has been staying with Benjamin as Scott and I have been bunking at the hospital, too.

My parents, Pam and Greg Jones, have also been a huge help with the kids. Not having to worry about Sara or Benjamin's well-being has been a tremendous weight off of our shoulders and all of the grandparents have done a great job of making sure Sara and Benjamin are not only taken care of but are happy, too. We could not have done this without them!

And tonight, last but certainly not least, is my wonderful husband: Scott. I would not have made it over these past few months of worry and uncertainty if it weren't for my very best friend whom I am lucky enough to call my husband. In times when I would get overwhelmed, he was right there with outstretched arms to provide the comfort and reassurance I needed to keep looking ahead. He has worked tirelessly to ensure that we are as financially ready for this as we could be to keep the burden from my shoulders. And during the end of this pregnancy and recovery from this birth, he has made sure that I want for nothing. I don't think I could possibly have endured this without him by my side. His love and constant presence have been exactly what I needed to make it. I am amazed and truly grateful.

Thank you, all of you, for the kind words and constant prayers that, I'm sure, are still going up as I type this. God is ultimately in control of this, as I've firmly believed from the beginning. Thank you, Father in Heaven, for the blessing of my child and for providing constant blessing through an experience that most will never see first-hand. Thank you for the strength and peace that have carried us all through. You are worthy of every praise that I can give.

Amen

Christopher's Story

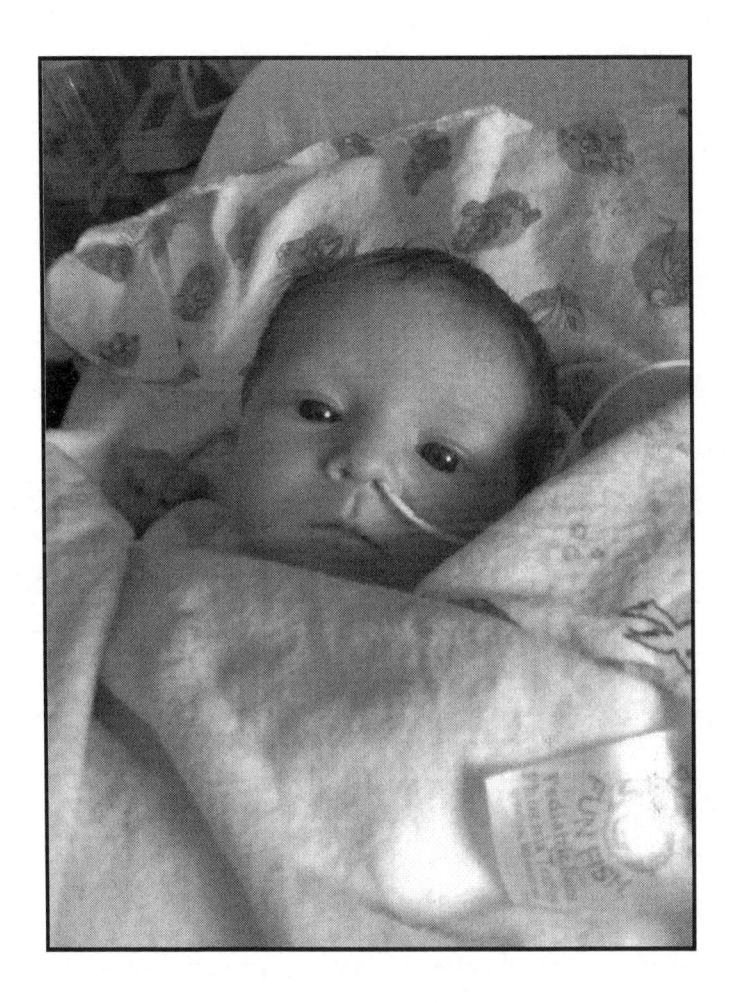

Friday, March 1, 2013

One Big Sigh of Relief!

Christopher is doing great! He is still requiring a few minor tweaks here and there to make the huge balancing act of his recovery work, but nurses and doctors have all said it's to be expected. He looks great, just sleeping. Scott and I actually got to kind of hold him tonight. By "hold him" I mean we were able to place one hand under his head and neck and the other hand under his bum and prop him up. It wasn't much, but we could have skin-to-skin contact and feel the weight of him. It was a small step in a very good direction.

Sara visited with a social worker who helps take care of patients' families. Since she was so upset at seeing her new baby brother all hooked up to tubes and wires, we were very glad to have the social worker talk to Sara about the difficulty that she had with seeing him. Margaret Kay is the lady's name. Margaret Kay used a full-linen doll to attach real IVs, tubes and sensors to explain to Sara what all of the different things do to help Christopher. Benjamin thought it was so interesting that he did one, too. When they finished, Sara could identify each part of the medical equipment and what it did. She even made a little purple line on the doll's chest to represent the incision where they opened Christopher's chest.

When it came time to leave the hospital for the day, Sara asked to go visit her brother. Originally we had decided not to let her see him again to avoid upsetting her any more, but we let her go in slowly letting her decide how close she wanted to get. She slowly approached his bedside and began to climb into the chair by his crib to get a better look. She wasn't afraid. She began to point at the IVs and sensors and telling us what each one did. The nurse, who has been phenomenal, talked with Sara and answered her questions. Sara even touched Christopher's leg and foot. It was truly a touching moment to witness. Priceless.

It's normal for parents to want to fix things for their children. A parent sees pain and wants to make to go away. I think it's natural. But some pain is beyond the help of a parent. I don't know if Scott or I had explained all of the equipment surrounding Christopher that day that it would have had the same effect as Margaret Kay and Kristin, the nurse, had on Sara or Benjamin. I think a child hears his/her parents so much that some things become numb to them. An outside perspective is needed. A valuable hospital staff member provides services outside of the scope of the job. The truly great ones do whatever is needed.

Kristin was our favorite nurse. She reminded Scott and me of a dear friend of ours from Florida named Djuana. Kristin was one of those nurses who talked to us like she had known us for years. Not only did she take phenomenal care of Christopher, but she would make sure we were taken care of, too. At the time Scott and I had put ourselves on the back burner and focused on our recovering infant. One of the most memorable and therapeutic moments in that intensive care unit was when Kristin told us a few funny stories about some things at Vandy.

"The docs got some new white coats with the logo embroidered on the right breast. The logo at the time was 'Nobody Cares Like We Do.' That was all well and good except many of the collars on the coats would cover up the 'Like We Do' part, so until a friend of mine pointed it out, doctors were walking around the hospital with a logo on their coat that said 'Nobody Cares.'"

Scott and I have a similar sense of humor and found this hilarious! Kristin was Christopher's nurse for several days during his stay in the PICU. All the while she made it as comfortable as possible for us all.

Monday, March 4, 2013

Making Continuous Improvements

Yesterday Christopher's breathing tube was taken out, but he had to wear a C-PAP mask like the ones adults wear for snoring sometimes. This mask wrapped around his entire head and face. Although it seemed better than the breathing tube, it made him very uncomfortable and VERY fussy! Scott and I were with him until almost midnight because we just couldn't leave him while he was so discontent. We took turns stroking his arms, holding his hand, talking and singing to him. He would quiet down momentarily but would get fussy again. Finally with the help of meds and probably exhaustion on his part, we were able to see him calm down enough for us to get some sleep.

This morning they took the C-PAP mask off and Christopher immediately became calm and peaceful. One tube was removed from his nose, so he only has the feeding tube left on his face. It is so nice to see almost his whole face! Scott and I got to hold him for the second time since he was born a week ago. He has been alert almost all morning with big dark eyes surveying the room. He has made barely a whimper and seems very content.

A speech therapist came in to evaluate how he would do beginning eating from a bottle. She had prepared a bottle for him with about ten milliliters of breast milk that I've been pumping and saving for him. Christopher has been taking a pacifier pretty well on and off as he was able, so she thought the bottle would work now. Scott held him while I held the bottle for him. He took it like a pro and then was rooting for more! The speech therapist was very satisfied and said that they would try to continue feeding him later today.

Scott and I are doing well. Yesterday was probably the toughest day so far. With the kids leaving with my mother and Scott's mother to return to Kingsport and Christopher being so out of sorts last night, we were pretty exhausted. Today, though, has been triumphant. We are seeing results of our baby boy's recovery as they take away IVs and tubes. Praise God for the good things and thank Him for strength during the tough ones.

By this time, Benjamin had missed almost two weeks of school. Benjamin was a sophomore in high school and Sara was in preschool. It was very important that Benjamin get back so that he didn't fall behind, and for Sara the importance was to get back into a regular routine. Being in the hospital for that long was taking its toll on them both. Our parents expressed on many occasions they would be willing to help however we needed. It was a tall order to fill, but both moms stepped up and took care of the other two we had at home so we could focus on our little one.

We were able to see just how important our involvement was in Christopher's recovery. Every bodily function was monitored so we could clearly see when we re-entered the room from going to eat or sleep Christopher's heart rate would improve and his breathing would be stronger. The connection between a baby and a parent is so physiologically strong. I didn't realize just how strong until I saw it for myself.

Wednesday, March 6, 2013

Graduated from PICU

A big milestone was reached today as Christopher was moved from the Pediatric Intensive Care Unit to a regular hospital room! This, of course, means that he no longer requires such

Christopher's Story

constant supervision from the nurses and doctors. This means two things: Scott and I will be much more involved with taking care of him and he is that much closer to going home.

I have actually become anxious the closer he gets to being discharged because his stats will still have to be watched closely until his next operation (predicted to be in June). Don't get me wrong; I will be supremely excited for our baby boy to come home and for all of us to finally be under one roof again, but I am nervous about his condition. It is a comfort for Scott to be a health care provider and to understand so much more than I do. I have been praying for peace about this all day.

Sara and Benjamin are doing well with the grandmothers taking care of them. They all seem to be settled in and having a good time with one another. We are grateful for the willingness of our mothers to take care of them as Scott and I are away for so long. Our friends and family have really stepped up in our time of need.

A big difference between intensive care and the general floor was that instead of a 1:1 patient to nurse ratio, it was more like 6:1. We finally got to do the normal parenting tasks of taking care of a newborn like changing his diaper and giving him a bath. There were still a few wires and tubes to work around, but we were getting used to that even to the point of picking him up out of the hospital crib and holding him in the rocking chair.

The most sensitive tubes were the chest tubes. A chest tube is a little smaller than a pencil in diameter and is inserted through the skin just under the ribs. The purpose of these tubes is to drain the blood and other fluid from around the heart that accumulates during recovery from surgery. Of course, Christopher could not tell us that these tubes were the problem, but since Scott had seen his sister Gladys have them after her heart transplant, he knew from what she described that the chest tubes were the worst. She had described them as "rubbing" inside her chest with every breath and movement. Knowing this, we were extremely careful when moving Christopher. Holding him took two people: one to pick him up being careful not to put pressure on his ribs as his sternum was still weak and healing and another to handle the tubes and wires connected to him. He could never be moved more than about two feet from the crib.

It was astonishing that he never fussed unless he was being messed with too much. The nurses kept calling him a rock star. I was ready to pitch a fit sometimes with all of the stuff that had to be done to him, but he took it like a champ. Maybe he didn't fuss because he had never known any different, but I like to think that he was just tough as nails.

Vitals had to be measured every four hours around the clock. This included taking his temperature, blood pressure—with a teeny tiny cuff that was so cute—measuring urine and fecal output through wet and dirty diapers, and once per day his weight was checked. Of all of these checks, getting his weight measured was the most unpleasant to him. He didn't like to be moved by the nurses and assistants. When Scott and I moved him to hold him, he didn't make a peep, but anyone else made him mad. When he got mad we didn't mind too much because that showed his spirit and spunk. Had he just laid there lethargically all the time, it would have been disheartening. His temper showed that he was a fighter. He was going to have to be.

Friday, March 8, 2013

Baby Steps

Things are steadily progressing with our little trooper. Today one of his two chest tubes was removed (a very uncomfortable part of his recovery), and he ate more from a bottle. Learning to take food by mouth is a bigger hurtle than I originally expected, but the speech therapist, who works with babies on this, said that he did exceptionally well. We have been told that many babies have a hard time even getting started in this direction, so she and the nurses were very excited to see this progress. His other chest tube is expected to come out tomorrow.

We had been told some babies were able to go home from the hospital weaned from the feeding tube, but many need it from the first surgery to the second. I had hoped that since he was doing so well, the feeding tube wouldn't be needed for long. It is called an NG (nasal gastric) tube because it is inserted through a nostril, down the esophagus and into the stomach. It is as unpleasant as it sounds, but Christopher seemed to get used to it. At this point we were still hopeful our little man would jump this hurtle and be tube free when we took him home.

During these long days of being in this hospital room, Scott studied for the MCAT as he was planning to apply to medical school. He had always wanted to be a doctor, but circumstances earlier in his life prevented this dream from coming true. There was a desk area in the room he used to toil over books for hours on end.

I worked on a new endeavor in book editing. A cousin of mine introduced me to a friend of hers named J.W. Holden who was interested in publishing some books, and he was looking for someone to edit and publish his material. He and I talked, and I decided to use the time in the hospital to get started on his first book. In between taking care of Christopher, we both worked.

Anyone who has ever slept in a hospital knows that "sleep" is a relative term. One might catch an hour or two of solid slumber, but mostly it is a constant barrage of hospital staff and medical equipment noises. Scott and I took turns staying overnight with Christopher. We figured that one of us should get a full night's sleep every other night. It worked out pretty well.

On the Heart Mamas Facebook page there were stories of parents whose marriages faced challenges in relation to their child's heart condition and all that entails. If anything, dealing with this life change served to strengthen our marriage. We were working as a team. Depending on each other was as important as Christopher's dependence on us. If we weren't working together well, then we couldn't do what we needed to for him.

Scott's time off was finite to the duration of the hospital stay. When we were discharged to go home, I would be the primary caregiver. This was the second time in my life that I have seen how God's sense of humor plays out. When I was seventeen, I said over and over, "I don't want to have children." I have five and I couldn't imagine not having each and every one. When I was making my career choice, some people suggested that a nurse was a good job. I said, "I can do a lot of things, but being a nurse is not one of them." Now I was to be a full-time nurse to my fifth child. Never say never.

The nurses taught me how to clean the healing wound that ran from the base of Christopher's throat to the base of his sternum. His breast bone had been split open for the surgery, so they taught us how to pick him up, not from under the arms even when his head was strong enough, but by lifting his legs with one hand and sliding the other hand under him to his neck to pick him up from his back. I learned how to feed him through the NG tube and how to administer his meds through it.

The worst part was inserting the feeding tube through his nose. It was not secured in any way except by strips of tape to his cheek, and the tube needed to be replaced periodically by a new tube for cleanliness. They taught me how to measure how long the tube needed to be inserted by holding the end just above his belly button, running it up and around behind his ear, across his face to his nostril. That was equivalent to how long the tube would be going in. Then I would get the tape ready to secure the excess tubing to his face. I used petroleum jelly to lubricate the tip of the tube for easier insertion. Then came the rough part. Running the tube into the nostril straight toward the back of his head feeding it hand over hand into his face until the premeasured point reached his nose. That's if it went well. Sometimes the tube would curl back towards his mouth after it made it through the nasal passage and come out of his mouth instead of going down his esophagus. The poor thing would gag and cough until I pulled it out to try again. It was best to surprise him so he wouldn't start vocalizing or shaking his head until I got it past his epiglottis. I learned quickly that his sneezing pushed the tube out of his nose and pulling the tube out made him sneeze. So sneezes brought me running.

Why all this discomfort and effort for the feeding tube? An infant's most taxing task is eating. It is what they expend the most calories and effort to do in their little lives, so a baby with a heart already working overtime just to circulate blood with half of its capacity needs no unnecessary strain on it. Therefore, any help he could get was good. Ideally Christopher would be strong enough even with the heart condition to be able to eat by mouth, but try as we might, he would not consistently gain weight in the hospital eating by mouth in order to thrive. So like it or not, the feeding tube was necessary for him to grow.

Christopher went home with a list of about a dozen meds to take multiple times a day. A few meds came with a weaning plan, but half of them would be with him until the next surgery at least. I felt like I was back in school and taking an oral quiz in science. The nurse who took care of Christopher the most often—her name was Brenna, and she was fabulous—gave me the list and explained what each medicine was for. I was not expected to remember the dosages, but I was expected to remember the name of the med, the frequency of administration and what the med did for Christopher. After I studied the list for a while, Brenna took Scott and me out into the hall and had me tell her the list and the details. Scott could have done it in his sleep, but I was the one in the hot seat because of my role in his care. I've never been so relieved to answer questions correctly.

Thursday, March 14, 2013

Going Home Soon

My apologies for it being so long since I last posted. Christopher has been hitting the milestones and goals set before him for discharge, and he is expected to be released tomorrow or Saturday! We are totally thrilled to be able to go home this soon post-op. He has done wonderfully and has captured the hearts of all of his caregivers here in Vanderbilt.

His care will be pretty involved until his next surgery, called the Glenn, in the series of three. The nurses have prepared us to know what we will need to know to take care of him. I never imagined that I'd know how to put a feeding tube in my child or be trained how to do CPR in case of the very rare chance he needs it. Honestly, I was pretty scared of the thought of all of this at first, but the staff here at Vanderbilt has made sure that we understand and are comfortable with what we will need to know and do for Christopher.

I have to sing the praises of this place. I have never seen a better healthcare establishment. Not only is everyone from the information desk to the surgery staff extremely knowledgeable in their respective jobs, but everyone here is overwhelmingly accommodating and polite. As uncomfortable as staying in a hospital can be, we have actually been pretty comfortable for the time we have spent here. The staff takes an interest in the well-being of the family members of patients as well as the patients themselves. There have been many commodities which we have enjoyed free of cost like food, laundry facilities, childcare, entertainment and sleeping quarters that help make staying in a hospital almost around the clock more bearable.

I would like to someday give back to Vanderbilt Children's Hospital to help them be as good to patients and families in the future as they have been to us. If you are ever looking for a worthy organization with which to make a charitable contribution, Vanderbilt is a great one.

The alternative procedure that allowed the surgery to be so much easier for Christopher's Norwood (first surgery) made his recovery a breeze compared to what we were anticipating. It was expected that he would have been on the heart and lung bypass machine during the Norwood procedure. Heart and lung bypass does exactly what it sounds like it does. The machine does the job of the heart and lungs for the body while surgery is performed effectively "bypassing" the body's actual organs and keeping the patient alive while the heart or lungs are operated on. It is astonishing and terrifying at the same time. Praise God our four-day-old son only required about half of the steps a regular Norwood procedure entails to make it to the Glenn (second surgery). We were told bypass was one of the most risky parts of these types of surgeries and it was very fortunate Christopher was able to avoid it. So he was tough to have recovered so quickly, but this was helped by the fact that he didn't have to go through such a tenuous part of surgery.

The grandmothers had been keeping Benjamin and Sara at our home in Kingsport for two weeks while Scott and I stayed with Christopher. Now the talk of going home was in the air. We had been in the dim, humming hospital room almost around the clock. We had actually fallen into a routine. We might have gone crazy if not for the comforts of the room. It was fairly spacious with a large window overlooking the roofs of the hospital. Most of the time we left the florescent lights off and just let the natural light flood the room. The ceiling tiles had yellow stars etched into them. We had our own bathroom and shower, and even though it was hard city water, it was nice to be able to bathe conveniently. While Christopher slept like newborns do most of the day, Scott and I toiled away on our studies and work. Scott sat at the desk mounted to the wall and I sat on the couch/bed with a rolling hospital lap table for my laptop desk. There was a television in the room, but we didn't use it much. Netflix on our smartphones was our entertainment of choice. Had it not been for movie streaming, we might have gone out of our minds.

Monday, March 18, 2013

Homecoming

Yesterday Christopher was discharged from the hospital and came home to his family. He was dubbed a rock star by all of the nurses who cared for him at Vandy because he rocked every milestone set before him. He was discharged far sooner than we ever imagined. It cannot be denied that God had His hand on this precious child. What we witnessed over these past three weeks has been nothing short of miraculous. To understand the magnitude and severity of Christopher's situation and to see him hurtle all obstacles is a testimony that I will carry with me for the rest of my life.

Although his recovery is incredible thus far, Christopher is not out of the woods yet. His fragile state is still not to be underestimated. Catching a common cold could hospitalize him again and be detrimental. As much as we want to share with our loved ones this new life, we will have to share it from afar until his Glenn (surgery #2). After that, he will likely be on parade for all who have taken such an interest in his plight. Please do not be offended by our aloofness; we simply cannot take a risk of exposing Christopher to illness unnecessarily. That being said, I want all of you to know yet again how much we appreciate prayers and encouragements that are still flooding in. As difficult as this has been, it has been such a comfort to have all of you in our corner. We thank you all so very much.

I have never been so happy to be at home. While my euphoria almost made me dizzy with glee, the gravity of having our fragile little one almost totally in my care now kept me on alert at all times. The nurses at Vandy taught me the basic care procedures, so I felt solidly proficient. Christopher had to be fed every three hours around the clock. I was also pumping breast milk as often as he was being fed. He needed such regular feedings to keep up with his body's caloric demand and to keep him from becoming dehydrated. Dehydration causes the blood to thicken and would cause his half-of-a-heart to have to work even harder to pump. It goes without saying this would be bad.

We had decided to forego the expensive feeding pump and feed Christopher through a gravity syringe. The part of the feeding tube from his nostril to the end outside of his body was about eighteen inches with a plug on the end to keep the contents of his stomach *in* his stomach where they belonged. The gravity syringe was a nine-inch-long tube with a tapered end that fit into the exterior end of the feeding tube. It looked like a huge shot syringe minus the needle. Like something a clown dressed as a doctor would use in a gag. In order to feed him, I had to attach the syringe to the end of the feeding tube, pour the breast milk/formula mix into the syringe and hold it above Christopher's head to let gravity pull the contents of the syringe though the feeding tube into his stomach.

That's how it went if everything went according to plan. One morning not long after we were home, I tried to feed Christopher the way I had been for several days. Before each feeding, I

Christopher's Story

had to "confirm placement" of the tube. To confirm placement of the tube I used a three-inch syringe filled with a little bit of air to push quickly into the feeding tube. While I did that, I listened with a very cheap stethoscope to my baby's belly for the *shuke* sound of the air passing freely through the tube and into his stomach indicating correct placement and no obstructions. However, this particular morning, I didn't hear the sound of the air. I heard nothing. The air didn't move through the tube at all.

This was not a time to panic just yet. Christopher was still taking a little bit of his feeding by mouth, so I was able to keep some fluids in him. But the tube needed to be fixed. After trying several times to reinsert the tube—each time being unsuccessful—I consulted with Scott and Christopher's pediatrician in Kingsport. It was decided that he needed to be taken to the hospital for an X-ray to confirm placement of the tube and to see if there was something else going on in his belly. I prayed that this would be resolved and that my son would not have to endure any more than necessary to fix this.

Nothing happens quickly in a hospital. We waited for the X-ray, and then we waited for the results all the while my stress level was slowly and steadily creeping higher. As the hours passed, I became more concerned about Christopher's hydration. We waited for two hours after the X-ray had been taken for the physician to tell us what she saw. With no way to feed my son except with my body, I nursed him. Scott and I had concluded that feeding him directly from my breast was a bad idea for two reasons: it was not the high-calorie mixture he needed and there was no way to know for sure how much he was ingesting. I did it anyway. He was willing to take it, and I knew he needed it. It had been too long and he was too fragile to let him go without anything. Something was better than nothing. So in that little room where we were waiting, I nursed my son for the first time since his birth the way God designed a mother to nourish her child.

"We will call you in a little while with the results," the physician finally came in and said.

"You can't tell me anything?" I was indignant. We had been waiting for so long and I was at my limit.

"I can see that there isn't an obstruction or kink in the tube, but I'm going to consult with another doctor when he is available."

"My son needs to be fed. He has a very strict feeding schedule because of his condition and I—"

"I'm afraid I can't tell you anything else right now. We will give you a call later today." And she walked out.

My head was spinning from fatigue, confusion, worry and anger. I left with my baby not knowing what to do. I wanted to cry, but I knew it wouldn't do anything to solve the problem.

It wasn't too long before I got a call from the X-ray technician. To protect his identity I'll call him Chuck. "The doctor can't tell you anything for sure, Mrs. Bontrager. I'm sorry," Chuck said sincerely.

"I've got to know what to do," I pleaded with him.

"Look—I'm not supposed to tell you this because I'm just a technician, not a doctor. But it looks like your son's tube is inserted too far into his belly and is actually coiled around once and inserted into the opening of the intestine. I'm not qualified to tell you this, but I know you're worried. I've seen this lots of times. Just back the tube out about two inches and it should be fine."

I was stunned and grateful. "Thank you! I'll try that!"

"Again, I'm not supposed to tell you this. Good luck," he said as he hung up.

I looked at Christopher who was asleep. I didn't like waking him up, but he was grossly overdue for his feeding. I untaped the end of the tube on his face, pulled it out the two inches that Chuck had suggested and secured it again to his cheek. I grabbed the stethoscope and air syringe to check placement. I held my breath as I closed my eyes and listened for the rushing air inside his belly. *Shuke*! It worked! The worry and stress of that day fell away like a cold puddle on the floor around me. What a simple fix! I couldn't believe that it was that easy. Thanks to an X-ray technician who overstepped his job description this problem was now solved.

Tuesday, March 26, 2013

One Week Home

It is so great to be home! Everyone has settled in to a routine. Christopher's one month birthday was yesterday and I find myself almost forgetting that he is a baby with special needs...almost. To look at him with clothes on you couldn't tell that three weeks ago he underwent major surgery. He eats well and is gaining weight, looks pink and healthy and is a pleasant little man. Then I give him a bath or change his clothes and see the thin, pink, two inch line just below his chin that is a staunch reminder that, yes, he only has half of his heart working for him. Before his birth everyone was praying for a miracle. I think what we all had in mind was that the doctors had made a misdiagnosis and that Christopher's heart would work normally. Of course, when that didn't happen it would be easy to think that the miracle didn't happen. I believe God did grant the miracle. The fact that this child is able to be fixed at all and that he's doing so well is, in fact, miraculous.

My biggest battle was feeding for Christopher. I hated the feeding tube. To me it meant he wasn't improving. As long as it was there, he was sick, and I so badly wanted him to be well. He ate by mouth moderately well for a few days, but the tube needed to go back in. He wasn't growing the way he should have, so I resigned myself to it.

Along with what the tube meant, it came with some difficult side effects for Christopher. The tube held his epiglottis open slightly causing some gastric disturbance. He spit up quite a bit at times.

The tape was another discomfort he had to endure because of the tube. The excess tube hung from just under his ear and was pretty easy to manage, but the part the came just out of his nostril had to be taped down. Anyone who has had tape on his/her skin for any length of time knows this isn't as easy as it sounds. A baby's skin is delicate especially on the face. I tried many kinds of tape before I found what worked best. Some tapes wouldn't stick and the tube would come out. Some tapes worked for a while until they got wet from a bath or saliva. Finally we found Tegaderm worked. It stuck and was pretty well water proof.

Reinserting the tube was a fairly regular occurrence. The older Christopher got, the better he could tell when it was going to happen. The smart little booger would start shaking his head when he saw the lubricant and tape. He hated it. I don't blame him. Poor thing. I felt so bad every time I had to do it, but I knew he needed it, so we got through it. When he was very small, I would swaddle him tightly to keep his arms from flailing. Then I would lube up the end, and down it would go. He would shake his head and cough and cry. It broke my heart every time. Scott helped when he could which made things a lot easier, but many times he was at work when it needed to be done.

The more dexterous Christopher became, the more he would get his finger through the loop of the tube by his nostril and pull it out. Of course, he had no idea what he was doing or I'm sure he would never have touched his nose. I got used to the signs of him pulling the tube out by the coughing and sneezing it would cause him as the tube was being pulled out. Sometimes I would get to him in time to stop him from pulling it all the way out. Other times, I would have to put it all the way back in. Socks on his hands worked for a while until he was able to take those off as well.

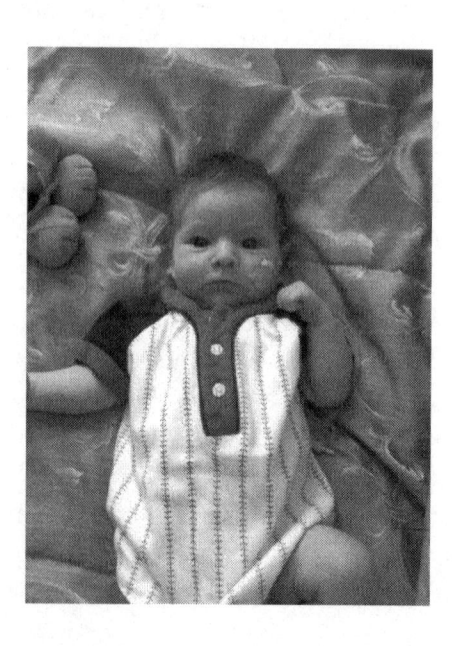

Tuesday, April 9, 2013

Six Weeks Old

The days pass very routinely now that we've been home for several weeks. Christopher is gaining weight steadily (an average of an ounce per day). He has filled out and is a very handsome little boy, if I may say so! He is staying awake more and more during the day and has begun cooing, which is utterly adorable! He is also sleeping most of the night, which is fantastic!

Christopher's cardiologist has given nothing but good reports about his heart function. We still don't have a definitive date for his second surgery (the Glenn). We have been told that the surgery date will be determined by how Christopher's shunt continues to work for him. As he grows, the shunt will not grow with him, therefore, when Christopher reaches a certain point in his development the second surgery will be necessary to maintain his heart function. We re-inserted his feeding tube to keep him from having to expend so many calories to eat (which burns more than I realized). After we did that, he started gaining weight much more steadily. Weight gain is important to the second surgery, apparently. We have been told that the more a child weighs, the easier the surgery and recovery are for him.

Not being able to have Christopher around people is not as challenging as I initially thought it would be. My days are quite full. However, I look forward to the time when we can take him to church or to the grocery store. Until then, Scott and I take turns going to church and running errands.

Sara and Benjamin are doing well and are excited about spring. Benjamin has taken up turkey hunting, and Sara looks forward to fishing with Scott and playing outside with Penny, our dog. They are both enjoying their baby brother. Benjamin likes to feed him his afternoon bottles when he gets home from school; he even offered to change a messy diaper yesterday! I, of course, happily accepted his offer! Sara has become quite good at helping to calm Christopher down when he gets fussy. One of her favorite things about him is that he grabs her finger and holds it while she talks to him.

Continued prayers are greatly appreciated and still necessary. As Christopher is doing well, we must keep in mind that he is still a very fragile little boy. We are not out of the woods yet, but I can see the clearing in the distance!

Sara was five years old at this time. She was to begin kindergarten the following fall. She took to being a big sister like a duck to water. Her personality is that of a nurturer, so she naturally wanted to help. I worried about her and Benjamin feeling neglected since their new baby brother required so much attention. As it turns out, they were part of the team that helped care for him. Neither of them are selfish people, so the graciously understood what needed to be done.

One of my favorite videos is one I took not long after we came home from the hospital of Sara and Christopher on the living room floor on a powder blue and brown quilt. Sara darned her pink plastic stethoscope pretending to listen to Christopher's heart. At barely a month old, Christopher watched her with the intensity of an older baby. He seemed to admire every move she made. "Yep, it's workin'," she said matter-of-factly.

"So you fixed him, huh?" I asked her playing along. I wouldn't let her see how deeply it touched me. She was pretending that his heart was fixed. I steeled myself refusing to let myself tear up.

"Yep. He can go home now," she added. She stood up and put her hands on her hips satisfied with her good work.

"That sounds great," I continued to humor her. All the while Christopher contently kicked and watched her.

Our days passed more easily as I got better at caring for Christopher, and we all grew accustomed to living with an immune-compromised baby. Any time any of us left the house for work, school, grocery store or whatever, immediately upon return showers would be taken to remove any outside contaminants that we might have come into contact with. Scott was especially cognizant of this as he was around sick people in clinic every day. Surprisingly, we all got used to it. It was what we had to do, so it got done.

Christopher was growing and changing like any other infant. Every day he was doing something new. His development was altered because of his condition. The most noticeable effect was his lack of ability to eat, but we had been prepared for his delayed physical development. The baby books that told of milestones needed to be forgotten because they just didn't apply to him. It would take him a long time to do things like roll over, sit up or walk, but we were assured that despite the delay, HLHS babies usually caught up with kids their own age by the time they began school. Christopher would just have to set his own pace.

Our little man's personality wasn't stunted by any means! His big, dark eyes were as expressive as any I've ever seen. I always thought he looked older than he actually was. His hair draped over his ears before he was three months old. Besides his physical features there was something about him that made him look like a more mature child. I chalk it up to what all he had endured at such a young age.

Friday, April 26, 2013

The Light at the End of the Tunnel

Last week Christopher was examined by his pediatric cardiologist here in Kingsport, Dr. Madhok. He has been doing so well that his next visit isn't scheduled for another two weeks from now. At the next visit Dr. Madhok will coordinate with Vanderbilt about the date for Christopher's next surgery. This is the one that will mark the end of the high-risk period of his situation! Unofficially, we are expecting this surgery #2 to happen at the end of June, but we will know more in two weeks.

Our efforts to keep Christopher healthy have been successful thus far. We appreciate everyone's patience and understanding with the situation. We know that there are so many who want to meet and greet this little guy, and we are looking forward to his "unveiling" at church and to the rest of the family and community.

The rest of us are doing well, too. Scott and I are doing well taking turns being at home with Christopher. We have a "tag-team" approach with church (he goes on Sunday morning and I go Sunday and Wednesday evenings). I get out and do the grocery shopping when he gets home from work. We even went for a whole-family picnic one pretty afternoon to the local state park since it was somewhere we could all go but not be around other people. Some have expressed concern for me being "stuck" at home all the time, but I don't look at it that way. I stay very busy taking care of Christopher and Sara, and I am working on editing projects. It might be more frustrating if I didn't know that there is a light at the end of the tunnel, but there is, so it's not.

Every afternoon when Benjamin gets home from school he spends some time holding and talking to Christopher. And every day Christopher gives his big brother tons of smiles! They are so cute together! Benjamin's school year is winding down, and he is looking forward to summertime. He has gotten a job mowing the lawn for a local church every week and seems to enjoy it.

Sara continues to be a huge help and a stellar big sister. She is very excited about starting kindergarten and spends time every day working on her math and reading workbooks. She and Scott are also working on staring a vegetable garden together.

Mary and Jolene are both excited to meet Christopher when travel is possible. We hope to have Mary fly down this summer and we hope to take a trip to Florida to see Jolene and see the rest of the family. Of course, our travel plans will all be dependent on Christopher's condition.

God has answered our prayers thus far, and we thank you for sending them up! We aren't out of the woods yet, but the clearing is near!

When Jolene was born, I was in college. She was born in March, so I took off the spring and summer semesters and returned to school in the fall. Never in my life up until that point did I have the desire to be a stay-at-home mother. I was career-minded and goal oriented. I guess because my mom had always worked, I didn't really consider staying at home full-time to be an option. I stayed home with Jolene for those months, but when it was time for me to go back to school, I was glad to do so.

Scott liked the idea of me staying home. When we moved to Tennessee, I did not find a teaching job right away, and the discussion of me being a stay-at-home mother was a viable option. Not that

I wanted to entertain it. I was a substitute teacher for the months before Christopher was born, but I knew that he would need me to stay home with him once he arrived. I never batted an eye. If putting my career on hold was what he needed, then so be it.

The days at home were not like before. They were filled with caring for both Christopher and the rest of the family. Besides taking care of our special needs little one, I felt that God was revealing to me the purpose of a woman. Chores became fulfilling as they never had before. Experimenting with cooking was a joy. Domestic tasks that seemed menial in the past were enjoyable.

• • •

One of the greatest parts of being a parent to me is the privilege of watching your children grow and change. Infants develop at a rapid rate. My dad remembers when my sister and I were babies that some days he would leave for work and by the time he got home he could tell that we were doing something new we were developing so quickly. Christopher was no exception. Although his strength was not increasing on the timeline of other babies, his personality was budding beautifully.

His smile lit up his entire face, and it was easy to make him smile. When Sara or Benjamin would talk to him, he would open his mouth as wide as it could go and squint his eyes he would smile so hard. It seemed to radiate from his hairline to his shoulders. His eyes were a strange deep blue color, no doubt still blue like many newborns. They were a dark ocean water color. I predicted that they would turn dark brown like mine, but for now, they were blue. And they were big. When he watched something, it seemed like he could look straight to the core of it. When he stared at something really intently like his vibrating lion toy or the end of his feeding tube which was a constant companion, he would appear to analyze it turning it over in his tiny fingers furrowing his brow in concentration, his mouth in a an "o" shape.

His fascination with our dog, Penny, was hilarious. Penny was a three-year-old Pudlepointer (sounds like "poodle pointer"). She weighed about sixty pounds and had chocolate brown, wiry hair. She was intelligent and loving, but not always patient. And Christopher was enthralled with her. We kept her in the house with us, and when she would be anywhere near him, Christopher would get that analyzing look on his face and reach for whatever part of her was closest. He would fondle her brown hair and pat her awkwardly. She tolerated his affections briefly but would usually find somewhere else to be out of his reach. She had never been around a baby before, and he made her nervous, I think.

Wednesday, May 8, 2013

An Estimated Date

I was anticipating knowing an exact date for Christopher's Glenn after his cardio check-up yesterday, but Dr. Madhok wants to have one more check-up visit before nailing down the appointment for surgery. What he *did* say was that he fully expects Christopher's second surgery to be the end of June. Everything looks great with him thus far, but the second surgery shouldn't happen before the four month mark because Christopher needs to be big enough to handle the procedure.

He has hit the ten pound mark and is already in three month clothes! It is exciting to see him grow. He smiles and is starting to laugh just a little. He isn't reaching for things yet, but he likes to look at the little snail character on the toy bar on his bouncy seat. He smiles at it quite a bit. He is especially happy in the mornings (not sure where he gets *that* from), and almost always wakes up cooing and smiling!

School is winding down and we are all looking forward to a very eventful summer! Prayers are still very much appreciated! God bless!

Every summer the kids and I make a trip to Florida to see our family. It was high on my priority list to make this trip. But even higher on that list was Christopher's safety. If the doctors said, "No, it won't be safe for him to go," then go we would not.

By this time, Christopher's personality was beginning to blossom. Newborns don't do much besides eat and sleep, but our little buddy was interacting with all of us by this point. Sara's play never directly involved Christopher as he was too little to participate, but she would acknowledge him often by planting a quick kiss on his forehead or letting him grab her finger as she walked by. I looked forward to the time he would toddle after her wanting to play for real.

Like most babies, our little man was happiest when he was being held. I got very good at doing my housework one-handed. I figured as much as he had already been through and what was still to come deserved much cuddle time. He was pretty good at holding his head up, but he was still a little uneasy, so it was hard to hold him constantly. I tried to fashion a marsupial wrap out of a sheet so that I could have him strapped to me without having to use my hand and arm so much. Unfortunately, it never quite worked. I found other ways to keep him near. I would carry him down to the basement in my arms to do laundry and on the way back up I would carry him in the basket full of clean clothes. His bouncy seat was on the kitchen table when I cooked and somewhere near me on the floor wherever I happened to be in the other parts of the house.

I wanted him near because it was a comfort to him and, frankly, it was a comfort to me. During this time—although our routine was well-established and becoming comfortable—I was never truly relaxed. It will be easier to portray this with a 1-10 scale. Level 1 is total relaxation, how one feels when no stress is acting upon one's self. Level 10 is full on panic mode, how one might feel inside a tornado. If one were to graph these levels as the events of the day progress, there would be spikes and valleys. My "at rest" level—the level at which no stressers were acting upon me—was around a 1 or 2 on average. With Christopher my "at rest" level never dropped below a 3 or 4. I still had the natural flow of spikes and valleys; the difference was now my senses were on alert all the time. Having him near was one way to put me more at ease.

Wednesday, May 22, 2013

Still No Official Date

We are entering the home stretch! Thus far things have gone smoothly for Christopher during this risky period in his young life, but there are still a few weeks left during this precarious time between surgery number one and surgery number two, so please continue to remember him in your prayers.

We were hoping to get a definitive date for the Glenn (#2) at Christopher's cardiologist visit yesterday, but we don't have one nailed down yet. Dr. Madhok has to collaborate with the team at

Vanderbilt, and the Vanderbilt team must meet on his case before anything is scheduled. However, Dr. Madhok said that there should be no reason to suspect the date will be any later than the end of June (as Christopher turns four-months-old on the 25th). His heart is strong, his overall health is very good and he is gaining weight like a champ. He is almost eleven pounds (birth weight 7 lbs. 10 oz.)! He still has his feeding tube in, but we feel like using it instead of feeding him by mouth has ensured his steady weight gain.

Summer kicks off Friday, and we are excited for an eventful one! Take care, everyone, and be on the lookout within the next week for a new post that reveals the date for the Glenn!!!

Wednesday, May 29, 2013

Official Date for the Glenn

We have an official date for Christopher's Glenn. We will head to Nashville on July 14th, he will have his diagnostic heart catheter on the 15th and his Glenn procedure will be on the 16th. We are told to expect him to be in the hospital for seven to ten days for procedures and recovery.

We had been expecting the second surgery to take place at the end of June. However, nothing about Christopher's condition is the cause of the unexpected change. The surgeon is simply booked up until the middle of July. We have been given no reason to be concerned about this change in schedule. It changes our plans for the summer a bit as well as those who are traveling to be here with us for the surgery but nothing more.

I must admit that I was displeased with this news as we were making further plans for the end of the summer along with our family coming to Nashville, but I've taken a step back from this to think. We have been put in the right place at the right time through all of this, and it has gone better than we could ever have expected. This too, although it seems like a negative, I have to trust to be in line with what God has in store for us. We have to keep on trusting, stay positive and have faith.

We are still super excited for the second surgery to be coming soon! Christopher still needs prayers. God has been with him through this fragile time, and I believe that He will stay with him always. When this precarious time comes to a close, we want to have a great big celebration! Praise be to God for He is good!

Tuesday, June 11, 2013

Doctors' Visits and Travel

In the past two weeks, Christopher has visited a pediatric gastroenterologist and his pediatric cardiologist. Both visits went well. He has had some issues with what we suspected was reflux, so we were referred to a doctor here in Kingsport to make sure there were no serious problems. Christopher continues to gain weight, so the gastroenterologist did not make any changes to his care.

We are planning to take our usual summer trip to Florida next week. I have taken extra steps to ensure that in the event of complications (Heaven forbid) that we have a very clear and satisfactory plan of action. We have been given clearance by all of Christopher's healthcare providers to take this trip. Of course, extra precautions will be taken to keep him from getting sick while we are visiting.

We want very much for all of our friends and family to meet Christopher and to introduce him to the world, but that is simply not going to happen at this point. Our visitors during our trip to Florida will have to be limited and even those who see him will have strict limits on access to him. It is overkill, we know, but that's just how things have to be. We are certainly not trying to hurt anyone's feelings, but Christopher's health is the top concern since he is still in such a fragile state. Everyone thus far has been completely understanding and compliant with our wishes, and for that we are *very* thankful.

All is well! God bless you all, our friends and family!

Truth be told, I was very *nervous* as well as very thankful. Mary, Benjamin and Sara are travelling troopers who make no complaints about long drives. No one could know how our new little guy would do with his special needs to boot. And I was making this journey with just Christopher, Sara and me, not Benjamin. We had flown him out to Idaho to spend some time with Mary instead of taking him to Florida. I was glad he got to go because he was so very excited to see her, but I lamented not having him to help with Christopher on the ten hour drive to and from Blountstown.

The plan was to stop twice on our way down. Our record is one stop in ten hours, but Christopher needed to be fed every three hours. Sara was nothing but helpful. She sat next to her baby brother and kept a watchful eye on him the whole trip. God has blessed me with five very unique children, and Sara's exceptional personality trait is her selflessness. She radiated that virtue on this drive more than any other time.

The trip went off without a hitch. We even made good time.

As I mentioned before, the last time I had seen Jolene around an infant was when Sara was born, so I wasn't sure how things would go. Children can be so different. My fears were put almost immediately to rest. At her first sight of Christopher, she walked straight to him and scooped him up bringing his head gently to rest on her shoulder. It nearly gave my parents and me a heart attack to see my eight-year-old pick him up and start moving around so confidently with him, but there was nothing to worry about. I don't think she would have let anything happen to him if her life depended on it. She took just as naturally to being a big sister to a baby as Sara did.

Usually our visits to Florida—or "home" as we still call it—are booked solid with seeing everyone we possibly can. Almost all of my family lives there and much of Scott's, so we make our rounds every year. This year was different. Only a handful of the closest family members came to see us as per my request. I asked that no one from outside of my parents' house touch anything except Christopher's feet and only them because he wasn't yet putting them in his mouth. I had taken such a risk bringing him down that I didn't want to compromise him any further. I also took other precautions. I made contact with a pediatric cardiologist in a nearby city

Christopher's Story

in case Christopher needed to be seen. I also called the local emergency response team to inform them of his condition and age. I had never heard of anybody with a condition like this, so I wanted the EMS team to be aware in case, God forbid, something went wrong.

Even the best laid plans have speed bumps. While we were down in Florida, I was called to come for a live interview with an online school based out of Orlando. Orlando is a six hour drive from Blountstown. We had a decision to make—me, Scott and my parents. I needed a job. This was a good one. But I couldn't leave Christopher for even 24 hours. There was no way to ask anyone else outside of a hospital to take care of him for that long and Scott was still in Kingsport. And then there was the question of the girls—what would they do? My parents stepped up in a big way.

Their generous offer was for my dad to stay at my parents' home with the girls and my mom to drive down to Orlando with me and Christopher and she would take care of him while I was in my seven hour meeting/interview. It is impossible to express how helpful this was. My relationship with my parents has had its ups and downs over the years, but they didn't bat an eye about helping me do this...until I demonstrated to Mama how to reinsert Christopher's feeding tube.

Proper preparation prevents poor performance, so I was showing Mama step by step how to feed Christopher. She had heard me tell her about it, and she had seen me do it many times during our visit thus far, but doing it by herself was going to be a whole new ballgame. My mother is a note-taker and a list-maker, so she had her hand-sized pink notepad out taking down the steps as I showed her. I also had to prepare her for the possibility of reinserting his feeding tube. Christopher had managed to keep his tube down for the few days we had been in their home, so they had not witnessed reinsertion. I purposefully pulled it out to demonstrate how to put it back in. Mama and Daddy stood over me as I knelt by Christopher on their green living room carpet, and they gaped at my demonstration. Even the smoothest of reinsertions were met with resistance from the little guy, and this time was particularly ugly. I wasn't trying to scare them, but it just didn't go very well. The tube came out of his mouth and he screamed and fought with all his might. When I finally got it down and taped to his face, I looked up at my horror-stricken parents. My immediate thought upon seeing their faces was, *Maybe I should try to reschedule this meeting*. But after the shock of the event wore off, my mother scrambled some courage from deep down inside and said, "I think I could do that if I *had* to."

And "had to" she did. While I was in my meeting, Mama stayed with Christopher in the hotel room we had rented, and lo and behold, he pulled the tube out! She told me the story later; she accounted that she just gritted her teeth, lubed up the end and down she pushed it. "I think I surprised him so much, that he didn't have a chance to fight until it was all done," she recounted.

"Atta girl, Mama! Now you've got a war story to tell!" I was trying to lighten the mood as she had clearly been rattled by the event.

"I hope I never have to do that again," she said looking down at the floor and shaking her head.

Other than the traumatic tube reinsertion, the trip to Orlando went off without a hitch. We returned to Blountstown and continued our visit. Scott even came down to see everyone. It was valuable time spent. Many of our close family got to see Christopher in the flesh who had not met him except through pictures and videos before.

Tuesday, July 9, 2013

One Week Pre-Glenn

One week from today our little man will go into the OR for his second surgery in the series of three. This one is called the Glenn. This surgery is not nearly as risky as the Norwood and will mark the end of the "high risk" period of Christopher's young life. We have been very careful and very lucky thus far in keeping him well. He is strong, happy and a healthy 13+ pounds!

He had a checkup today with his cardiologist here in Kingsport. This was one last visit before the

Glenn to make sure everything is going as expected. It is. His heart sounds good, and he is growing the way he should.

With the expressed blessing of Christopher's doctors, we made our summer trip to Florida to visit Jolene (who is doing so very well and growing into a smart, sweet, beautiful young lady:). She was so very good with him, and he smiled every time she spoke to him! It was so great to see her! All went very well. A few close friends and family were invited to meet Christopher (all taking special precautions to keep him cold- and flu-free). It seemed to make everyone feel a little more at ease about his condition. He is a very happy baby, and aside from the feeding tube, he looks like any other boy his age. I think in the back of everyone's mind Christopher was this fragile, sickly infant. In fact, he has done incredibly well despite his circumstances. He fits his "Lionheart" nickname to a T.

We are very lucky to have brought my mother-in-law Annette (Granny) back with us from Florida. She will be going to Nashville with us next week where we will meet my mom and dad who will be there for the duration of our stay. Annette and my parents have been amazing to us through this whole ordeal. I don't know what we would have done without their help.

We pull out for Nashville on Sunday, and Christopher is expected to be in the hospital for 7-10 days. The heart cath will be Monday and the Glenn is Tuesday. I will be posting very frequently throughout his journey.

If you will bear with me for a moment, I will make a little promotion. For this surgery, Christopher will need four units of blood for the transfusions necessary to make the surgery a success. I realize that blood donation is time-consuming, uncomfortable and inconvenient, but for situations like his and so many others, it has kept him alive. I, myself, have not donated as often as I should, but every time I do I know that it's going for a good cause. It is even more important to me now. If you have a chance, your donation can help save someone like Christopher who would not survive this extensive surgery without someone's (several someone's) blood donation.

Sara is doing well and enjoyed her trip to Florida to spend time with JoJo. Benjamin is visiting Mary in Idaho for a few weeks, and he and Mary have plans to fly to Nashville while we are there to bring Benjamin home and for Mary to stay for a visit. We are looking forward to having our other kiddos home!

Starting at the beginning of next week, watch Facebook for updates about Christopher which will be frequent as he goes in for phase two of the reparation of his hypoplastic left heart. Thank you and God bless!

The Norwood was supposed to be hard for Christopher; it was easier. We had no idea the ride our baby boy was in for.

Monday, July 15, 2013

Cath Lab

Christopher is in the cath lab for a very low-risk procedure. It should last about three hours after which he will stay overnight in the ICU. Next update will be when we are notified that they are done. The doctors and nurses said he looks GREAT! It was hard to hand him over, but he is on his way to getting fixed!

We sat with Christopher in the pre-op area caressing, cuddling and talking sweetly to him. He, of course, had no idea what he was in for, but we did, and we hated sending him off for yet another procedure. The cath lab doctor was the one who came to take him into the cath lab which we thought was an unusual task for an MD. For the first surgery, Christopher was wheeled in a hospital crib to the operating room, but this time he would be taken by the doctor himself. "This is my favorite part of my job. I get to carry the little ones to this procedure," he told us as he smiled down at our little boy. Christopher smiled back.

I can't remember the man's name, but I'll never forget that doctor picking Christopher up with great care and turning to walk with him down the hall toward the cath lab all the while looking down at the baby in his arms talking to our little one. *That's one of the things that makes this place special,* I thought. *To these people this is more than just a job.*

Cath is Done

He came through the cath wonderfully, and no extra work needed to be done to prepare for tomorrow. He is now headed to the ICU for recovery and observation tonight as per standard procedure because he was put under anesthesia. We will see him in about half an hour.

Tuesday, July 16, 2013

The Morning of Surgery

We are here seeing Christopher before he goes back for surgery. He is "first case" so they will get started at about 8:00 am. We have been told to expect the surgery to last 4-6 hours, so he is in for a long day.

Everyone keeps saying how great he looks and what a fighter he is. The following blogs today will be frequent and short. Nurses will give us updates from the OR about every hour. Thank you for your prayers! God has His hand on our little Lionheart!

7:00 am

We walked Christopher to the doors of the surgery wing, and now he is in the hands of Vanderbilt's fantastic staff. The greatest comfort is he is and has always been in God's hands. Pray on!

As hard as it was to send Christopher off to surgery at four days old, sending him off this time was ten times harder. Scott and I did not want to leave his side. It was heartbreaking to send him off as a newborn, but now we *knew* him. He wasn't just our offspring, he was a family member who had a personality with his own sounds and likes and dislikes. Christopher was calm as they wheeled him down the hall in the hospital crib for surgery, but for a few minutes Scott and I stood in the hall holding each other with tears running down our faces.

Now, the waiting. Thank God we didn't have to sit in that third floor waiting room for the whole surgery. They contacted us again by cell phone so we could move around the hospital and surrounding neighborhood, never far. But we met our friends and family who were there (my parents, Annette, Sara, Pastor Tom Legg and his wife Lynn from our church). All of us were tense.

8:30 am

They are going in.

9:45 am

They are "working through the layers" and things are going well. Not on bypass yet.

11:00 am

He is on bypass. This is the big part of surgery. The climax.

Christopher was being kept alive by machine. I felt like vomiting. Of all the parts of the procedure, this was the part that was the hardest on his little body. His anatomy had allowed bypass to be avoided for the Norwood, but now it was necessary.

12:30 pm

We have crested the hill of the climax. All of the repair work is finished and they are starting to take him off bypass which is a process. Everything looks good but to know for sure that everything is working well they have to "turn the water back on" to see that the plumbing is working the way it should. They will call us back within an hour.

1:45 pm

It went great! Everything is just like they expected! Praise God! He will go to ICU in 30 minutes and we will see him about an hour after that!

I didn't post what happened next in my blog. I was too frightened and distracted. After we got the notification at 1:45, Scott, Sara and I went around the corner to a legendary pancake place to finally eat—we hadn't been able to eat much before. We were told that things were going fine and it would be a while before there was anything for us to do, so we felt safe to leave the hospital grounds.

While we were eating, Scott's phone rang. He answered and his face fell. Over his plate of pancakes he just kept acknowledging whatever the person on the phone was saying. When the call ended, he looked at me wide-eyed. Sara was with us, so he tried to be delicate. "That was the OR nurse. Something is amiss. They have to go back in. They'll call back in a little while to let us know how it goes."

Christopher's OR nurse was the same Justin Long look-alike that Christopher had for his Norwood. Scott told me later he knew the situation was bad when the nurse told him, "I'm praying for your little boy."

The jovial, celebratory mood was gone. I stared at my plate of half-eaten pancakes not knowing if I could keep what was already in my stomach down. I prayed. Then I looked around the crowded restaurant and thought of asking others to pray, but I couldn't move. Scott and I called our parents to give them to unnerving news. When Sara finished her M&M pancakes, we went back to the hospital waiting room.

About an hour later, we got another call from the OR nurse saying that they thought they had fixed what was wrong and Christopher was being closed up again. He also said they would watch him for a little while in the OR to make sure everything was okay.

Another call. They were closing him up and things looked good.

6:00 pm

We finally got back to see Christopher. He looks the way we expected him to, much like last time. The biggest part is over; now the recovery is up to him. He has lived up to his Lionheart nickname thus far, and I expect he will continue to be a fighter! More tomorrow on his recovery, but not as frequent. Thank you for all the words of encouragement and comfort and most of all for your prayers on our family's behalf.

I really sugar-coated this. Christopher looked awful. He looked like he had been hit by a truck. He was swollen to almost twice his normal size. I took a picture of him with my phone. I thought he might want to see what he had looked like when he got older. Words can't express what he looked like.

Wednesday, July 17, 2013

Bump in the Road

They suspect a blood clot in the artery that takes blood to the left lung from the heart. The next step is to get him back into the cath lab to take a better look at what's happening in there. He is very stable now. And since he is a work-in, he won't get into the cath lab until 5:00 or 6:00.

He had a peaceful night last night. The numbers are just indicating that something isn't quite right. No one is getting overly excited, but they are working on getting it fixed.

He's not out of the woods yet. Please keep lifting him up in prayer!

Cath #2

We are expecting him to get into the cath lab at about 5:00 pm. He is stable and peaceful. That's the scary part of a blood clot, though. And that's why Vandy is the big leagues because before this gets to be an all-out emergency they will head it off at the pass! God, please lay Your healing hands on my boy!

In Cath #2

He's in the cath lab. What they find will determine how long he's there. If it's a clot, they might take it out with the cath or they might do more surgery to retrieve it.

It is possible it's a constricted vessel. If that's the case, they may try to stretch the vessel or they might just wait for the swelling to go down and let it stretch on its own.

Whatever the outcome we are assured we will know some answers soon.

Cath Results

Cath is done. Went well. No blood clot. The problem is a restricted vessel. Not completely blocked, just restricted. It will require surgery to go back in and repair it. It will be done within 24 hours. Possibly tonight. Not the best news, but far from the worst!!!

Surgery Tomorrow

Just got word that the surgery is set for 7:00 am tomorrow. This surgery isn't nearly as risky because they are working on a vessel, not the heart itself. We haven't been back to see the little guy since the cath, but we are told he's fine. I will update y'all in the morning when we get surgery started. Whew!

Thursday, July 18, 2013

Nurse called. Things are going exactly as expected. Doing well. We will get another update in an hour to 90 minutes from now.

Finished!

Done! Surgeon is very confident that the shunt they put in will fix the issue. Wow! What a day! Prayers are being answered as I type!

Christopher's chest had been opened three times within 72 hours! It is only by the grace of God he survived.

Back in ICU

We are back in the room with him. His numbers are good. The nurse said that whatever they did seemed to work and he's doing fine. (Collective sigh of relief.) I will update y'all in the morning. You can assume that no news is good news tonight. Thank you all for standing and praying with us.

Friday, July 19, 2013

Is It Really Friday?

An uneventful night. And if we can keep him out of the OR, I will consider this day a success. This is the time that all of the numerous support meds and devices should start being taken away as he recovers. They have already taken a med away and other signs say he is looking good. Today they are working on removing excess fluid (he is very puffy) and letting him rest. I hope I will give you one more update tonight to let you know how swimmingly it's going. Again, no news is good news. I will enjoy having a lower level of tension for the first time in four days! Thanks, everybody!

Uneventful Day

The term "uneventful" is relative. There are things constantly happening with Christopher but nothing like opening his chest twice in one day! Gosh, was that really only yesterday? It seems like a week ago. Time means nothing here. There is no need to know what day of the week it is or whether it's morning or evening. The only reason to know the date is for the purpose of signing in to the Ronald McDonald waiting room (you can feel good about donating to that charity, by the way). Other than that, the day is filled with nurses, tubes, beeping, ticking, doctors, ventilators and germ-xing your hands three dozen times a day.

Our little Lionheart is making progress. A few support lines have fallen away because he has healed beyond needing them. He has a ways to go, but every tube pulled out, every monitor turned off, every medicine discontinued is one step closer to taking him back home.

Scott and I took Sara for an outing for a few precious hours today. Even with her stellar attitude, we could tell that being in this hospital for so many days was taking its toll on her. We took her to see *Despicable Me 2* which she enjoyed immensely! She cackled through the whole film. We needed the outing as much as she did.

Mary and Benjamin arrive early Monday morning, and we are so very excited about that!

The journey is not over, but we have crested the hill and are on our way to getting our baby boy back home where he belongs. Praise be to the Lord, for He is good and has made His love and power known!

Saturday, July 20, 2013

Day 2 Post-Op(s)

Swelling has gone WAY down! Christopher looked not unlike the Michelin Man for the last few days. Of course, that's to be expected when one has had his chest opened up three times within a 72 hour span. I don't know about y'all, but that sounds like science fiction coupled with a horror movie. He's tougher than anybody I've ever known to have come through that!

He's still sleeping, but he tries to open his eyes when he hears a familiar voice. They want him to start moving around soon. Seriously? I hope these poor nurses know what they are in for. Our little man is quite the kicker, and the spaghetti labyrinth of IVs and tubes is in for quite a tangling! We will see how that goes.

I expect to give another positive update later this evening!

Saturday Evening

Another blissfully uneventful day! Yes, things have been happening, but they are little things, and they are all headed in a positive direction. A few more support systems have been weaned. The nurse tried to take the breathing tube away, but he just wasn't ready yet. She compared taking him off of the ventilator to running to get into shape when you are out of shape. On day one, you can only run for two blocks without getting too tired. Then day two, you can run for four blocks, and so on, until you have worked up to having your lungs in shape enough to run a marathon. Christopher's lungs must get back into shape before he can go without help breathing. She also said that some swelling needs to come down to make it easier for him to breathe.

There are dozens of little support systems and meds for him to come off of, but the biggies are the breathing tube and the chest tubes (which are most unpleasant according to adults who have had them). Today he has been wiggling his feet and legs and trying to open his eyes. He looks like he's been on a three day binge when he opens them, but that's the narcotic haze. The best part of today to me has been that he grabs our fingers. He grips and holds and will make little squeezes when we talk to him. He is still drugged up to make the pain easier to handle, but he is coming back to us. We can see our baby boy again.

I'm watching your prayers being answered! God is good!

Sunday, July 21, 2013

Sunday

When I came in this morning, he was awake! His eyes were still hazy because of the three pain meds being pumped in to him, but he is very responsive and conscious!

They did the "see if his lungs are in good enough shape to go off the ventilator" tests last night, and he did well. Goal is to extabate today! Yay! Huge milestone!

I'll let y'all know if and when the tube is removed today. Have a great Sunday, and God bless:-)

Extabation Complete

Breathing tube is out, and our Lionheart is doing great! Very big step in recovery!!!

Without the breathing tube, we could see his little face! It was a huge comfort to us, but having that tube out of his throat was an extreme relief for him, I'm sure.

Progressing Quickly

Not only is he breathing on his own with no issues, but he has been moved to a step-down ICU room where each nurse tends to two patients instead of a 1:1 ratio. He doesn't need such constant care!

His meds are dropping away. He has dropped four just today. He did have upwards of 12+ through his IV, so the improvement can actually be quantified in lost meds. He is being fed now. Before his first feeds yesterday, he hadn't been fed since 10:00 pm last Sunday.

He has been awake intermittently today. When my dad came in, he spoke to Christopher and the little man tried to smile at Daddy. When he is awake now he looks around at whoever is with him. As of yet, he has not been fussy at all, which surprises me! He is usually a very happy baby, but when he is ticked off, he is a firecracker! I guess after the week he's had he doesn't sweat things like his foot being poked to get a glucose reading.

While we are celebrating our troubling time coming to a recovering close, there are so many others here who we have talked to who are not as fortunate as us. I've heard of a child who was mauled by a pit bull; Marien, a baby who was life-flighted here after almost dying when she was only a few days old; Veronica, a nine-year-old girl with a debilitating bone disorder who will be in chronic pain and never grow above three feet tall. Veronica has been in this hospital for months and will likely be here on and off for the rest of her life. And there are babies with Christopher's condition who are not doing nearly as well as he is. I'm praying for so many children that I've seen that I can hardly keep track. I guess my point is that we should all be thankful for the good things in our lives. As I pray and feel sorry for these kids and their families, I thank Him for all of my healthy loved ones. It's a very sobering reality check.

The doors to individual patient rooms along the halls to Christopher's room were usually open. As I would walk down the hallway to Christopher's room, I couldn't help but glance into the opened doors to see the kids inside. The children were of all ages and ailments. Many of the older children would be sitting up in bed. More often than not, the child's head would be bald. I'm guessing the heads would either be shaved for a cranial procedure or the child had lost it due to chemotherapy.

A child is beautiful no matter if he or she has hair or not, but I have heard from cancer patients who have lost their hair that hair loss can be traumatic. My hair is important to me, but I've always thought that losing it because of chemo wouldn't be the worst of the situation. Benjamin and I were talking one day about this very subject when he said something extremely insightful for a young man his age.

"The stress and fear of cancer is probably too hard for some folks to handle. So they get upset about losing their hair instead because it is easier to get over that." I was stunned at the identification of transference that Benjamin articulated.

My hair has been my thing for a long time. I have kept it long for many years, sometimes as long as my waist. I try to take good care of it. When I was in my early twenties, I cut ten inches off to donate to Locks of Love. I just felt led to donate it. Now in Vanderbilt Children's Hospital, I felt led again to donate my hair to help a child endure the traumatizing fight to live.

I made an appointment with a hair stylist not long after we got home from the hospital. She told me that she had cut and sent off hair to Locks of Love many times and that she would take care of sending it. There wasn't much else I could do for these poor kids whose rooms lined the halls of Vandy. But I could give my hair. I prayed that it would be a blessing to someone who needed it.

Monday, July 22, 2013

Monday

Christopher is still in ICU and still steadily progressing. His color looks so much better than before surgery. The next big step will be removal of chest tubes. I am told that we can expect that to happen around Wednesday. The move up to the general patient rooms from ICU will be another big step towards going home. No word yet on when that will be.

Scott returned to Kingsport yesterday, unhappily, to work today and tomorrow. He will be back with us here in Nashville on Wednesday, but he is not happy at all about being away from Christopher. Constant text updates do little to satisfy the want to be here with our little man, but he's doing the best he can.

Sara is coping pretty well. She is growing a little bored even with all of the fantastic accommodations that the children's hospital has to offer siblings of patients. I'm hoping that issue will be remedied when Mary and Benjamin arrive tomorrow morning. She hasn't seen Benjamin in five weeks since he's been out in Idaho visiting

Mary, and she hasn't seen Mary since Thanksgiving! It will be exciting for her to see them again.

Mary is beside herself to meet Christopher, and Benjamin is on pins and needles to see his baby brother again after so long. Tomorrow should be a good day for all. God bless and thank you for praying so diligently!

Wednesday, July 24, 2013

Wednesday

There have been baby-step improvements over the past two days. A med discontinued here, a tube removed there. He is steadily being weaned from the multitude of supports.

I have found that many people are concerned about Christopher's feedings. This isn't as big of a concern to me because I've been so used to him having a feeding tube all these months. I know he won't go hungry because he is being helped with feeding. On the front of eating, however, the speech therapist has come by and given a plan for reintroducing a bottle. For the rest of the time he's here at Vandy, the speech therapist will work with him to get him to begin taking a bottle. We will likely go home with a schedule for a speech therapist in Kingsport to come to the house to continue working with him until he is proficient with his feeding. He won't starve! I promise!

Mary and Benjamin have been here since yesterday, and they were so happy to see their baby brother! Sara has been overjoyed to have them back, too! We are all growing weary of being away from home, but as long as Christopher makes constant progress, we are thankful!

Having Mary and Benjamin with us made for a more eventful schedule for us. While most of each day was spent in the hospital, we made it a priority to have dinner somewhere together every night Mary was there. We did a few touristy things around Nashville as well like visiting Music Row. One day the kids went to the Nashville Zoo and had a blast.

Vandy brings in all sorts of special events for the patients and families. While we were there they had family movie nights with pizza; Nashville's professional hockey team (the Predators) came to visit; and some miniature horses were brought in! Mary and Sara are both horse crazy, so Mary took Sara down to the lobby where the horses were to see and pet them. These miniature horses were the size of medium-sized dogs. Mary took a picture of Sara with one and the horse's back came to Sara's hip. They thought it was so cool!

Thursday, July 25, 2013

Day 11

We are still in ICU but only because there are no rooms available on the general floor. He is ready, though. Good things are happening, praise the Lord!

Scott took the kids to a water park today which all of them enjoyed! We are still managing to have a good time despite the circumstances.

Scott and I never slept in the ICU with Christopher, but Mary decided she wanted to. She knew she would only be in town for a few days, so she wanted to be with her new baby brother as much as possible. During the times that Christopher was sleeping, she would sit in the back of the room and watch Netflix, but any time he was awake or the nurses were doing something with him, she would be at Christopher's side holding his little hand and talking to him. It seemed like they got to know each other even though this time they had together was fleeting.

Saturday, July 27, 2013

Day 13

We moved out of ICU yesterday AND had the chest tubes removed!!! Two very big steps towards recovery! Prayers are still needed and appreciated. We are winding down our stay here at the hospital, hopefully. God bless you all, and have a good Saturday!

Little did we know, Christopher's time for this hospital stay was only half-over. The night after this post, Mary and I were staying in the general floor hospital room with Christopher. In the middle of the night, we awoke to a crowd of doctors and nurses surrounding his crib. They were talking over what was happening and what needed to be done. I was in a total haze from lack of sleep and couldn't understand what they were saying. I did comprehend that we were being moved back down to the ICU. Mary and I got up and packed our things to make the move.

Christopher had had trouble with spitting up almost all of his life. The formula just didn't seem to agree with his stomach even when it was mixed with breast milk. A few weeks before, he had to go on formula completely because I was no longer able to produce breast milk for him. His spitting up—projectile vomit at times—was a minor thing until now. His emesis (medical term for evacuation of the stomach) was frequent now and difficult for him. Whoever was with him would sit him up so that it was easier for him to get it out, but aspiration (inhaling it into his lungs) was always a concern. Not to mention, it was heartbreaking to see him struggle so. Also, he was still on oxygen with the two pronged tube in his nostrils because his blood oxygen level was not stable. He had made great improvements, but he was struggling.

Monday, July 29, 2013

Day 15

Christopher is back in the ICU. At 1:00 am today his breathing was brought up as a concern, and after doctors assessed him, it was determined that he needed to be moved back to intensive care for more consistent observation. In ICU the patient to nurse ratio is 1:1 or 2:1. On the general floor that ratio is 8:1. Between Christopher's gagging and vomiting not being explained and him not coming off of oxygen like he should have, doctors didn't feel like he was ready to be on the general floor yet.

It was discovered that the top portion of his right lung looks like it has collapsed, and they are working to fix this by giving him a treatment that makes him breathe in very deeply to help expand that lung.

The cause of his gagging and vomiting is unclear. There are a couple of hypotheses: 1) acid reflux, which he has a history of (this is the most likely guess); 2) he is not feeling well, getting very fussy and gagging himself; 3) the antibiotics he has been on are making him sick to his stomach. Whatever the reason, those in the ICU are watching closely to pinpoint and correct what is ailing the poor child.

The good news in all of this is that his heart is doing great! There has been no cause for concern about anything being wrong with that system. We keep plugging away here in Nashville. Please keep Christopher in your prayers. He is a strong little boy, but he has been through so much in the past 15 days. Our little Lionheart will continue fighting!

A fourth possible cause of Christopher's emesis as we came to discover later may have been narcotic withdrawal. The step-down from pain medications for babies in this situation isn't normally too hard on them, but Christopher's situation was different. The extra surgeries he went through called for the need for extra pain meds; therefore, it is possible that he had become dependent on them and essentially was going through detox. I have never understood why anyone would deliberately get hooked on something like that, and seeing my son go through withdrawals was almost more than I could stand.

Tuesday, July 30, 2013

Hiccups

It has been an eventful morning, but with all that I'm updating you on, the doctors have assured us that nothing that's happening is a big surprise.

When Scott and I walked into Christopher's ICU room this morning, eight doctors and nurses were surrounding his bed. If you've ever been in or with someone in the ICU, you know that isn't a comforting sight. Christopher's breathing was much labored. After an X-ray and an ultrasound of his lungs and heart, it was determined that his heart function is wonderful. The shunt is working the way that it should, and they are very satisfied that the issue does not include his heart. Whew! Okay. On to his lungs.

The images they took showed fluid buildup between the left lung and the chest wall. They have some guesses as to how it got there, but they said it doesn't matter at this point because the treatment is the same to remove it. They inserted another chest tube on his left side, but this one is smaller than the others and is supposed to be less irritating. The tube has already drained off 25 milliliters (or ccs) of fluid, and he is breathing *much* more easily.

They are continuing to feed Christopher into his intestines instead of his stomach. He has not had any more issues with vomiting or seeming uncomfortable because of his belly. Since the lungs are a much more immediate concern, the gastro issues have been put on the back burner, so to speak. Heart? Check. Lungs? Check. Tummy? Hopefully addressed next.

We were concerned that these bumps in the road were abnormal for HLHS kids and that Christopher's case was atypical. A doctor sat down with us and told us that these hiccups he is facing are not surprising at all. We were just very spoiled with Christopher's first surgery, I guess. Everything went so smoothly in February that we expected him to knock this surgery out with no problems. What is happening now is what many others face. It doesn't make it any easier to see the hiccups happen, but it does do something to comfort us knowing that they see this stuff happen all the time with HLHS kids. They've seen it, and they know how to fix it.

Thank You, Heavenly Father, for being with us through these trials. Thank You for the health that our little boy *does* have. And thank You for providing a way to repair his body.

We came to find out the recovery issues for Christopher's first two surgeries were inverted from what was first projected. Usually these issues come with the first surgery and the second surgery is a breeze comparatively. But Christopher was now going through the more difficult one for his Glenn instead of his Norwood. This is because of the "hybrid" layout of his anatomy. So basically, the hard one could be put off until he was a few months old and stronger and hopefully better able to handle it as opposed to when he was four days old. I suppose that is a good thing. I don't know if he would have been strong enough to survive all of the complications that he faced if he had been through them as a newborn. So I thank God for the conditions that allowed the tough one to be postponed.

Wednesday, July 31, 2013

Day 17

Christopher acts like a different baby today than yesterday! As tense as yesterday was, today was delightfully relaxing. He has drifted in and out of naps which he so desperately needed. The chest tube is still draining fluid, but the diuretics are doing their job in keeping him "dry". Being "wet" is what they refer to when fluid builds up (like around his lung yesterday).

They started feeding him again since his lung issue is stable. He is being fed NJ which in layman's terms means that the feeding tube is run down his nose, through his stomach and deposits the formula into his small intestine. Doing this allows for the food to bypass the stomach making it easier for him to digest what he is fed. Of course, he can't intake his food this way forever, but until they are sure his respiratory issue is resolved, they want to cause as little disruption to his overall condition as possible while still giving him the nourishment he needs to live. The next step is to increase his NJ feeds to "goal" which means a full day's calorie intake; then they will move the tube to NG. "NG" means that the tube will go down his nose, into his stomach and deposit the formula there. This is how he has been fed all of these months at home. Once they see that his stomach can handle digestion, we will move to trying to take a bottle. Again, baby steps.

Mary flew back to Idaho today. She made it just fine. It was so wonderful to see her, but I'm sure she was glad to get home. She spent all of her time here with us in Nashville, many nights with me in the hospital including the night that they moved Christopher back to the ICU at 1:00 am. Despite the circumstances of her visit, we still managed to have a great time together as a family.

Scott, Benjamin and Sara have gone back to Kingsport (much to Scott's chagrin). Benjamin and Sara start school on Monday, so it will be good for them to get back into a routine at home before embarking on a new school year. It is Sara's first day of kindergarten on Monday, you see, so this is all very exciting and a little nerve wracking to her. Being home will do them some good. Scott wanted so badly to stay, for obvious reasons. My mom and dad are still in Nashville with me, and I'm grateful for that. We are all doing the best we can, and we will continue to do so. There is no other option.

"No temptation has overtaken you except such as is common to man; but God is faithful, who will not allow you to be tempted beyond what you are able, but with the temptation will also make the way of escape, that you may be able to bear it." 1 Corinthians 10:13. All I can say, Lord, is "I'm flattered."

I missed Sara's first day of kindergarten because she started while I was still with Christopher in Nashville. Scott was there with her, but it broke my heart to miss it. I'm grateful for such an understanding family.

Thursday, August 1, 2013

I Can't Believe It's August

This year has been a blur. People have asked me how I have managed not to be a nervous wreck all the time with all that's happened. I tell them that you never know what you can handle until you are faced with it. Now, I am in no way relaxed...ever. There is a constant level of tension that is higher than at other times in life. That level is manageable and invisible to most, but it is there; it is always there. It falls on the scale directly between total serenity and mental meltdown. It has become the norm. And, as others know who have found themselves in the crises of real life, my faith has held me and my family up. If we could not find solace in God's mercy and love, we would all have lost it long ago. When I pray, it feels like weight lifts from my shoulders...so I pray A LOT!

Yesterday and today have found my youngest child a whole new person. He has smiled, kicked, played with toys and flirted with nurses. I dare say he is the most popular kid on the floor. He makes everyone who walks through that big sliding-glass door smile with him. The chest tube is still draining, the feeds are still increasing and the oxygen will hopefully come off tonight. And in more crude news, he has had a bowel movement (you may have no idea how important that is, but it is great news)! All systems are go!

Scott and the kids are keeping busy at home. They will be back here in Nashville soon. We still have no idea when we will be OTD (Out The Door, as one doctor put it), and I don't ask for fear of getting my hopes dashed by a longer stay. We will all be back home together soon. God knows when. I feel that He is teaching me lessons in patience, so I bide my time and do what I can where I am. How did August get here so quickly this year?

Friday, August 2, 2013

Day 19

It was decided today that Christopher is ready to go to the general floor, but there is no room available right now. Until a room becomes available, he will continue to hang out in the ICU making an easier shift for whoever his nurse is. I have been told on several occasions that he's the cutest, sweetest baby on the floor. I try to be humble, but, yes, I concur. :)

Sunday, August 4, 2013

Day 21

We hit another speed-bump last night. After I left Christopher, he threw up nine times. Just when we thought this stuff was under control. It really has been a roller coaster ride for the poor kid. During rounds (when the doctors on the floor meet outside of each room to discuss the individual cases) the doctors decided to get some questions answered by the gastroenterology team (GI doctors). I was glad to hear that. The good news during rounds was that

Christopher's heart and lung function are doing great. The last time he had bouts of vomiting a week ago he also had fluid built up around his left lung and had to have another chest tube inserted to drain it off. That is not the case this time. The problem seems to be isolated in his belly.

The GI team came to his room here in the ICU not long after rounds. The plan of action is to first try to double his reflux medicine. Since he has a history of reflux issues, they thought reflux might still be his problem now. If that doesn't work, they will try changing his formula to something that is "more elementary" in content. In other words, "easier to digest." If that doesn't work, they will run a scope through his nose into his esophagus and belly to have a look. An ultrasound of his belly has also been ordered since that is a non-invasive way to look around. I am thankful for a plan of action. Very clear treatments and contingencies.

My mom and dad are going home to Florida tomorrow. They have been here with us since day one, and we have been very grateful for their help and support. We never expected to be here this long, but they wanted to stay until everything was stable with Christopher and with me. I am confident that he will be fine, and I know I will. As long as I have Netflix and a place to lay my head (and, Lord willing, a shower) I will hold out quite a while longer. I'm determined to hold out, and I'm just stubborn enough that I'll do just that!

Monday, August 5, 2013

Moved Upstairs...Again

Christopher is no longer in ICU; I say this while wincing because he's been here before only to be taken back to intensive care for breathing complications. If this hospital stay has taught me one thing, it's that nothing is certain. I have been relieved a whole handful of times over these past three weeks only to have the breath knocked out of me when something sets Christopher back. Each setback has been less severe every time, but I still hesitate to celebrate just yet.

He has done very well today, though. He has enjoyed this afternoon being in his own room without the noise and activity of the ICU. He has slept for most of it.

The speech therapist finally came by to do the "swallow study" today which is when she watches as I give Christopher a bottle with about 10 milliliters (or ccs) of formula. That equals about 1/3 of an ounce, so it is a tiny amount. As I offered it to him, she watched for things like latching the nipple, speed of suction, formula spilled, jaw movement, and swallow movements in the chin and throat. I expected him to turn the bottle away as he has so many times at home, but to my shock and excitement, he took all 10 ccs in about 60 seconds! I was speechless! Ironically, so was the speech therapist! (I had to say it.) The plan is to offer him small amounts through the bottle a few times a day. He is still being fed NJ (into the small intestines) so as to give his stomach a chance to benefit from the increased reflux medicine. As he succeeds, the bottle will be offered more and more. We can be discharged before he is totally on the bottle, so thankfully that won't keep us here even if he decides not to take it well again.

"Today was a success," I say with bated breath.

My family was gone, and my parents were gone. It was just Christopher and I in Nashville. I can't say that it was lonely, because there were always lots of people around, and I can't say it was boring because there was constant care to be given to my little man. I was so very sick and tired of living in that hospital even as nice as it was. I was sick and tired of it for Christopher, too. He had been doing so well at home, and I kept thinking of Scott's words: "People get stable in the hospital; people get well at home."

Wednesday, August 7, 2013

Day 24

Talk of discharge wafts through the air. Christopher has a few goals to meet before he can be OTD (Out The Door). He must make one more increase of calories in his formula, take feeds every four hours instead of a continuous pump and receive all of his meds by mouth instead of by IV. He must do all of this while gaining weight. He has had some bouts of reflux spit-ups last night and today, but overall he is in a very good mood.

Sleeping at night is a challenge for both me and Christopher. Last night someone came into the room every two hours. Each time Christopher was woken up and difficult to calm down. By 6:00 this morning I was not a happy mama. Our day-nurse who came on at 7:00 am realized what had happened. She was pretty put out that the night staff had scheduled tasks so poorly. She took one look at me and said that she was putting a sign on the door that read "See nurse before entering patient room." She said that she wouldn't let anyone mess with us until we were both rested. Her demeanor was not unlike a Rottweiler guarding her domain. Because of this Christopher was able to sleep undisturbed for the rest of the morning.

I'm usually a polite person; I value good manners and I never want to hurt anyone's feelings. But on this morning, I was pissed! (Please, pardon the expression.) My son was recovering from major surgery! He needed rest, and the hospital staff was not giving it to him. Around the clock they would stick to their schedules no matter if it was good for him or not. Vitals, X-rays, meds, bedclothes changes, etc. These have to be done, I understand, but they do not need to be done every two hours. Christopher would be woken up and barely go back to sleep before the next interruption.

At 5:00 in the morning a poor medical student came in. This med student had been in several times before, always at the same time. What was annoying was he moved loudly through the room and talked with his voice at normal conversational volume. He would wake Christopher up with all of this then want to examine him. Christopher was always irritated to be examined after being woken up. So the guy would disturb my baby, make him mad and then want to *discuss* things with me about him. The logical side of my brain knew this guy was just young and insensitive to the emotional plight of a patient. I knew this medical student was just trying to learn the way he had been trained, but this kid needed to be taught a lesson in etiquette, and that morning, I was his teacher. Christopher and I were both asleep when the med student opened the door—loudly, of course. I sat straight up and glared at him. His eyes met my bagged ones, and I held up my hand for him to wait. He stopped halfway through the door. I got up from my couch/bed and walked to him in my socked feet and gently pushed him back through the door. With my hair a mess, no shoes and wrinkled clothes I said, "Listen, we've had a rough night, and this is a very bad time for you to come in here. My son hasn't gotten more than an hour's worth of sleep at one time all night, so when and if you come back, you'll have to see him when he's already awake. And when you do come back, be aware that this is not some office that you're working in. Some of us have been here for a while, so this is our home for now. Respect it and enter like you would someone's home, because as well as a hospital room, that's what it is." He looked shocked, but he did what I told him and left.

He came back later that afternoon. He knocked at the door and waited for me to say, "Come in." He peaked his head through the door and without a word looked to see if Christopher was awake. Indeed he was. The medical student entered, did a brief examination, asked a few questions and thanked me for our time. He had taken the lesson to heart.

Saturday, August 10, 2013

Day 27

Yesterday Christopher tolerated his feeds well all day. Today the plan changed to bolas feeds instead of continuous. "Bolas" feeds are more condensed feeds that are more like a normal feeding schedule where the stomach is fed all at once, empties and is filled again several hours later. There was still a question of whether Christopher would handle this new feeding schedule, but so far he has done well. He had one bolas feed earlier today and is halfway through one now. He still gets a bit fussy, but I'm not sure whether to chalk it up to sleepiness or discomfort from reflux. It is entirely possible that he is cranky because he has been in a hospital for twenty-seven days. Lord knows that's the catalyst for my fussiness.

The discharge date will likely not be Monday, but rather the new expected OTD date will be

Tuesday. I can't say that I'm surprised by this. When we were here in March for Christopher's first surgery, discharge went very similarly. The date we were given changed several times due to changes in how Christopher handled things. I am resigned to the fact that I will believe we are going home when I walk out to the parking garage with Christopher in tow. Even then I will be looking over my shoulder to be sure that some nurse isn't running after me saying, "Wait, we have one more goal we have to meet!" Please pray for a calm belly and a restful night for Christopher.

Monday, August 12, 2013

Day 29

Still working on belly issues. Christopher seems to tolerate his night feedings much better than his daytime feeds for some reason. He is still gaining weight, but a good amount of his fed formula comes back up. It is not unusual for babies to spit up. It has been explained to me, though, that the reason it is so important for Christopher to keep his formula down, aside from the fact that he needs to gain weight, is to keep him from becoming dehydrated. Dehydration would cause vessel constriction and possible blood clots, neither of which Christopher can risk with his shunt.

On top of everything else, it seems that Mr. Christopher has begun teething in the middle of this ordeal. He has been pretty fussy today, and I didn't even suspect it until the nurse asked if he had begun cutting teeth. Upon feeling his gums, I found that they were pretty swollen and the bottom front teeth feel like they are going to break through soon. It isn't comfortable for the poor kid, but at least it explains why he is difficult to console over the past few days. I do have a teething ring, and I've given him a cold, wet washcloth to chew on, but he's just plain uncomfortable.

The first estimated discharge date was today...then they said Tuesday...now they are saying Wednesday. If we get to go home before this weekend, I will be grateful. Please pray for Christopher's belly issues and overall comfort. Anyone who has had children knows how teething can take its toll on a child. At twenty-five days after a series of three open-heart surgeries, "discomfort" is a gross understatement for my little man.

Despite all of these issues, our little Lionheart still manages to smile at those around him. Not at everyone and certainly not all the time, but there are moments when he shows that million-dollar grin that lights up his whole face. He's the toughest person I know.

Tuesday, August 13, 2013

Day 30

I'm gonna give myself permission to get a little excited...they've said we are being discharged tomorrow! The last of the milestones have been met, and he has had a very good day. Very little fussiness and very little emesis (that's medical lingo for puking). All systems are go!

Final ultrasound of the heart and belly look good. He still has an IV line in his leg which will be taken out right before we go home. That line hasn't been used in several days, but they like to keep an access line available while he stays in the hospital just in case meds have to be administered quickly. He continues to gain weight as well.

I'm under no delusions that discharge will happen first thing in the morning. They know how far we have to drive to get home, and they want to make sure to get us out of here at a decent time of day. I expect we will be pulling out around lunch time. Over the four hour drive to Kingsport Christopher will have to be fed, and I will be able to do this easily with a feeding pump that runs off of batteries that we are being sent home with. Some people have expressed concerns for how I will handle this. I drove with him and Sara for a ten hour trip earlier this summer on our visit to Florida. I've got this! We will be sure to take it easy, and we will be safe.

Please continue to lift those prayers Heavenward. Our little Lionheart has done well despite his setbacks, but he still needs the healing Hand of God. When you think about it though, don't we all? We all have something to bring before the Almighty, but if you have our baby boy in your prayers, we'd sure be grateful still.

I was so used to taking care of Christopher by now that I did almost all of the care for him in the hospital even though we had wonderful nurses there to help. I wanted to. It felt more like home for me to do those things for him like feed him and give him his meds. But it wasn't home. He seemed well for the most part, but he was still not keeping food down like he should have been. His belly had become the problem, not his heart. I wanted badly to go home, but I wanted even more for my son to be well.

I don't know if Christopher felt as cooped up as I did, but in my imagination it was driving us both crazy. He was still hooked up to monitors, so mobility was an issue. One of the nurses offered me a portable monitor to use to take him out of the room and around the floor of the hospital. Going outside still wasn't an option, but I was able to hold Christopher and walk him around. I even commandeered one of the little red wagons from downstairs in the lobby to move him around. It was nice to walk and make laps around the hallways. My little guy seemed to like it. His big, dark eyes drank in the colors and people that we passed. When a nurse would stop to speak to him, he would give his great big smile. It melted hearts, that smile.

As the days passed and we actually managed to fall into a routine of living in the hospital, the day came for us to go home! I didn't want to believe it until I held the discharge papers in my hands. Of course, I had been packed for hours before we actually left, but we were on our way! It would be just me and my little man, but since we had already made the trip to and from Florida, this four hour trek would be a piece of cake.

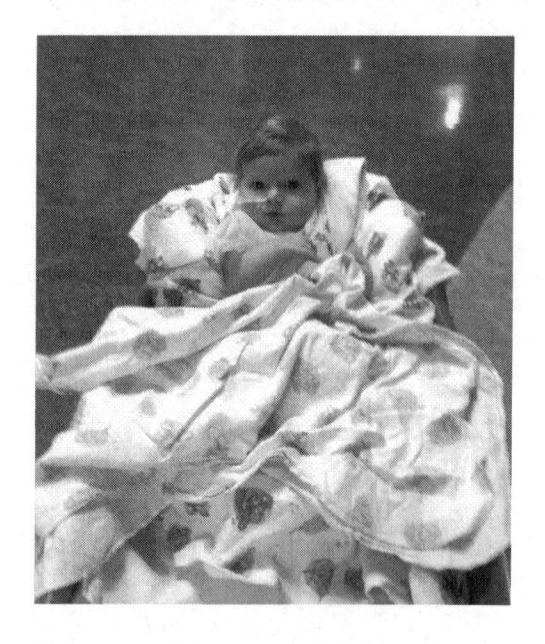

Riding around the hospital hall in the wagon.

Wednesday, August 14, 2013

Day 31

Forgive the short post, but WE ARE HOME!!!

I relished the simple silence of being at home those first few days. We basked in the privacy and comfort of home. Christopher seemed happier, and I know I was. Finally we could get on with our lives, and now we had the possibility of public interaction. I was excited about this. We could finally introduce our son to our church family and get out into the rest of the world. But we still needed to remain isolated for a few more weeks while he made a full recovery from the horrendous nightmare that was his Glenn. The last thing he needed after enduring that ordeal was to be exposed to something that could set him back.

Thursday, August 29, 2013

Blissfully Home

Yesterday marked two weeks since we returned home from Nashville. For the most part things have been sailing smoothly. We got the go-ahead last week from Dr. Madhok, Christopher's cardiologist here in Kingsport, to get Christopher out and around people. I went straight from the cardiologist's office to Walmart. I've never had so much fun shopping for groceries. And Sunday we introduced him to our church family. It was a joyous day, indeed! It also happened that we had a church picnic Sunday afternoon for several baptisms, so the entire household had a wonderful time socializing and enjoying the beautiful Tennessee outdoors.

Honestly, I expected things to be easier this time coming home than in March when Christopher was discharged from the hospital. As far as his care goes, it is actually more involved now than it was when he was a newborn. He has a small pharmacy's worth of medication to take several times per day, and his feedings remain challenging. It's a source of great stress for me. It just hurts me all over when he can't "keep his cookies down" as we say, trying to make light of his spewing. Despite frequent spitting up/vomiting, he *has* managed to gain weight and does not seem to be dehydrated. I continue to be grateful for his healthy heart and lungs.

Scott is having his gall bladder taken out today. He has had symptoms for quite a while, but he has put himself on the back burner because of Christopher's condition. He did not allow me even to take him to the hospital. He doesn't have much of a choice about being picked up, though. Driving post-op and barely post-sedation is more than even *he* can handle. Luckily, his procedure is laparoscopic and out-patient, so no more nights in the hospital for anyone. And since this weekend is Labor Day weekend, he has four more days after today to recover. I have a feeling that ready or not come Tuesday he will slip on those slacks and tighten that tie and head off to work whether it is what his doctor recommends or not. I've learned that that's how healthcare workers are. They don't always make for the most compliant patients.

School is going very well for Benjamin, Sara and Jolene. They all seem to like their teachers. Sara loves school, and sometimes seems to have a little too much fun, even when she's not supposed to. We've gotten feedback about some very minor misbehavior such as playing in her pencil box and talking to friends when she should be working, but she understands her error and quickly corrects herself the following day. All in all, she's having a ball. Benjamin is liking not being the low dog on campus this year. He comes home talking about the lowly freshmen. My, my, how quickly our perspective changes our attitude. I find it amusing. Jolene seems to like her teacher. I've never met Ms. Webb, but Jolene says she enjoys her class very much. Third grade. I can't believe it!

Sara and Benjamin are both playing soccer. Sara's first practice was Tuesday, and she suited up in her pink and black cleats and shin guards. It was too cute! Scott is going to coach her team which I find fantastically cool! I was watching them practice and was surprised to see that Sara was one of the tallest kids on the field, and she was playing with five- *and* six-year-olds! How did *that* happen?! She was doing great! Benjamin sat out of sports last year. He's been playing since he was Sara's age, and he just didn't have the fire in him to play anymore. He seems excited to get started again, though. His first practice is tonight.

I didn't realize I had so much to report until I sat down and began ticking away at the keyboard. A lot has happened in two weeks. I have to admit that it has been very nice not to have to do this every day. Thank you to everyone who has followed our journey and prayed for our little Lionheart. God bless and have a good one!

Being able to take Christopher out changed the dynamics of our family quite a bit. Now he could be a part of what was going on with the rest of us, and so could I. Going out to lunch after church with friends was an event that I looked forward to. Christopher rode in his stroller onto the soccer sidelines with his feeding pump strapped to the handle for feedings. Life was still complicated, but it was more normal than ever for him in his young life.

Feedings were still a great source of stress for me. I wanted that feeding tube gone. We had been told after the second surgery he would be stronger and better able to handle eating on his own. We were supposed to be out of the woods. Instead, we had begun seeing both an occupational therapist for small motor skills and feeding and a physical therapist to try and help Christopher catch up developmentally. I had been spoiled by how well he had done after the first surgery and I still had high expectations for him. I wanted the best for him, but I still watched him struggle.

Thursday, September 26, 2013

Seven Months Old

Christopher turned seven months old yesterday. It seems like much longer ago that we met him in that crowded operating room and began what has been the most frightening journey of our lives. The big stuff is over for now. The latest cardiology exam was extremely positive with heart and lungs looking and sounding great! Currently, Christopher's challenges all involve his digestive system. From his mouth to his bum, we have worked with his belly constantly.

Thankfully his spitting up issue is totally under control. Believe it or not, the answer to his vomiting was switching him to goat's milk! Nutramagin (the formula he's been on from birth) is supposed to be the gentlest formula you can use and is even specified to use with babies with a cow's milk allergy. We have no reason to believe that Christopher is allergic to cow's milk; it's just what they started him on from day one. We tried another formula for sensitive bellies, but he didn't keep that down either. Anemone, a friend from church, suggested that we try goat's milk since she's had several babies with similar problems thrive once they switched from formula. She has goats and offered to give us the milk that she got from the one that is lactating. We decided that it was worth a try. From the very first day we started the little guy on the goat's milk, he kept it all down! Since beginning it, he's had to have some formula to supplement the goat's milk because he needs a few more calories than what goat's milk alone provides, but I guess the formula added is so little that his belly still agrees with it. Whew! Finally! The poor kid can be fed without tossing his cookies!

I was *extremely* impatient with the fact that Christopher still has his feeding tube. I was under the impression that the tube would be gone shortly after bringing him home from his Glenn. I am very disappointed that he still has to have it. I also feel like I was misled by doctors and nurses who made it sound like post-Glenn that the tube would just not be needed anymore. Since the spitting up is under control now, I'm not in as much of a hurry to take the tube out as it doesn't seem to be the cause of his belly discomfort; however, the tape used to keep the tube in place on his cheek makes his face very raw-looking. He doesn't seem to be in much pain from it until the tape comes off, but it looks painful. Anyway, until we get Christopher's weight gain consistent, no talk of tube weaning will commence. I'm introducing baby food to him as you would any other baby (a different one every week), and he is doing pretty well with that. Just takes a little at a time for now, but at least he's taking it. I am disappointed to still have the tube, but the cost of taking it away is that he doesn't get the nourishment he needs, so the tube it is.

Sara and Benjamin are right in the middle of soccer season. Sara runs her heart out and is learning so much from her Daddy who is her coach. Benjamin is enjoying the season far more than he expected to, but last week in a collision with two other players on the field he threw out his right knee. He's been on crutches since the accident. An X-ray showed his femur has a small fracture and his LCL ligament is possibly torn. He got an MRI yesterday, so we hope to hear good news from it in the next few days.

And life goes on! Autumn is in the air here in the Blue Ridge Mountains, and we all keep on truckin'! Have a great one, thanks for praying, and God bless!!!

By the time our friend Anenome offered the goat's milk to us, I was desperate. I had researched on the internet about feeding problems to little avail. I had brought my concern to his doctors who offered a few suggestions, but for the most part as long as Christopher was gaining weight no one was alarmed. Well, I was. I watched him day and night struggle and I couldn't take it anymore. Something had to be done or at least tried to help my son. He had gone through too much for this problem to be ignored. So in desperation, I tried the goat's milk. It was given to us raw, so I pasteurized it myself. I still had to add the formula, so almost every day I looked like a mad scientist in my kitchen with a food thermometer and mixing stations set up for preparing my little boy's milk. He was trying to eat baby food by mouth, but he took so little at a time that the solid food couldn't be counted on to provide even a little of what he needed.

The goat's milk worked! Even Christopher's doctors were pleased that it was working. I was afraid that they would be against it, but since he seemed to be improving with his digestion, they were okay with it. The only drawback was that his lower digestive track wasn't doing as well. He became constipated after being on the goat's milk for several days and sometimes needed help with bowel movements. One end was happy while the other was not.

Thursday, October 3, 2013

Reality Check

You know how I've said in the past that it's sometimes easy to forget what a fragile state Christopher is in...well, Tuesday was a cold splash of reality to remind me that, yes, his heart condition still exists.

Over the past several days, Christopher had developed a cough. Nothing else but a cough. Then Monday morning he woke up looking puffy around his face, especially around his eyes. The puffiness subsided, but when he woke up with the swelling again Tuesday morning, it was time to take him in to see his doctor.

What made the day so stressful was having to get Christopher's blood drawn. Even if he didn't have his heart condition, he is still very small and apparently inherited my hard-to-find veins, so he is an awfully hard stick. It took two trips to two different phlebotomists and three sticks to finally get a good draw. After getting the good blood sample, we weren't sure what was going to happen next. It was possible that Christopher would have been checked into the hospital if the results came back showing the need. The good news was that the questionable levels came back normal. To fix what was happening, he needed a diuretic to draw off the fluid build-up.

The fluid built up because his heart is not keeping up with pumping for his growing body. I was concerned about what this meant for Christopher's heart function in the future. I wondered if fluid build-up would always be an issue for him, but Scott said that once he is more mobile, his legs will help his heart out with the pumping of blood to the lower half of his body and help with the distribution of that fluid. All in all, a concerning problem with an easy solution.

As far as Benjamin's leg is concerned, the MRI showed no tear in his knee. We were all relieved, but none as much as Benjamin. He is now back to 100% knee usage. Good news all around!

The "puffiness" was a symptom of congestive heart failure. When Christopher was diagnosed with congestive heart failure, I was very upset. I discussed it with Scott when he got home that afternoon from work.

"That sounds terrible! Doctors shouldn't call it something like that. It makes it sound like his heart will quit working." I was in denial about how grim the diagnosis actually was.

"Well," Scott said thoughtfully, "that's exactly what it is. The heart isn't pumping like it should, so fluid is building up causing the cough and making it harder for his heart to pump compounding the problem, and if it isn't fixed, his heart will fail. It is a perfect title for the condition."

He was explaining it as best he could, but he didn't want to frighten me. Our little man was in trouble, and I was ignorant to just how severe his condition could be. I had it in my mind that he would be fine. He had made it through the toughest part of his life, or so we assumed.

Christopher's cough worried Scott and I both. Any baby being ill is worrisome to a parent, but we were on high alert for our little boy.

Thursday, October 10, 2013

Doing Much Better Now

After over a week of close monitoring of Christopher's weight and more blood work, he is doing much better. The swelling has gone down, his cough is gone, and he is a much happier little boy.

Later today Christopher will have his first visit to the occupational therapist. He will also be going to physical therapy next week. I had no idea that an infant could have occupational therapy and from what I understand OT will work with fine motor skills, which Christopher is doing pretty well with, and PT will work with larger motor skills such as sitting up. At seven months old Christopher still does not sit up on his own. He can hold himself up for a while in his Bumbee chair (a hard foam seat contoured to fit around his legs, hips and back supporting him slightly as he sits up), but he doesn't do well at all without support. I'm excited to see how physical therapy will help him. Friends of mine who have had special needs children in PT have said that it is hard work for the child, but it pays off.

The feeding tube is still in. My next step is to try to contact someone at Vanderbilt to get some help with weaning. There isn't anyone in Kingsport who has been found to help. It is an exercise in frustration to research tube weaning online. I have introduced all of the step one baby foods to Christopher. He still doesn't take a bunch at a time, but his favorite seems to be apples. We will keep working with eating, but I'm just thankful that he's gaining weight, growing and seems happy. We have so much to be thankful for!

Between this post and the last one, much happened.

I took Christopher to both occupational therapy and physical therapy. He hated them both. He particularly hated physical therapy, but he only went there once. He cried from the moment the therapist touched him until I put him in his carrier to leave. I think the strain was just too much for him. He didn't mind the occupational therapy as much. We worked on his eating and hand movements. He still did not like another person besides me touching him and having him do things.

The swelling from the congestive heart failure improved for a few days, but then it came back. He would wake up with the most noticeable swelling being in his face. The cough returned as well. To compound the CHF, Christopher also contracted a cold. A true cold this time. Runny nose and difficulty breathing. At about 10:00 pm on Friday, October 18th we couldn't wait any longer. He had rapidly gotten worse. We had a decision to make. Have a doctor that Scott worked with make a house call to assess Christopher, or take him to Niswonger Children's Hospital in Johnson City twenty miles away and check him in through the emergency room. We decided to go with the hospital. I packed an overnight bag for Christopher and me, and Scott stayed home with Sara and Benjamin.

Christopher was assessed in the ER, and we were finally checked into an intensive care room at around 2:00 am. We were told by hospital staff that he didn't need to be in the ICU, but all of their general floor rooms were full. We settled in for what was left of the night. Here we were again. Just me and my little buddy in the hospital.

For the most part, Christopher was left alone by the hospital staff. The only thing that was out of the ordinary was that he needed breathing treatments. We had to stay in the hospital until his blood oxygen level (O2 sats) stayed consistently within normal range. His were too low. He had all kinds of monitors, an oxygen cannula in his nostrils and an IV in his arm. He looked more bound up this time than he did in Vandy. I sat by his bed and watched the O2 sats almost constantly. The number would briefly rise to normal range and would fall again to a dangerous level. Christopher's heart simply wasn't keeping up with what his body needed.

He was in Niswonger Children's Hospital for four nights. Scott, Benjamin and Sara came to see him and to bring more goat's milk and changes of clothes for me. Christopher slept much of the time.

His last night in the hospital, Christopher woke up and was alert for quite a while during the evening. I found the movie *Cars* for him to watch. I thought he might enjoy it. His color looked good; his eyes were bright. I thought we were on the downhill stretch of this setback. I took a picture of him while he watched the movie. The picture captured the essence of my son. He only wore his diaper. His right arm was wrapped in a splint to secure the IV. His feeding tube and the nasal cannula wound around his face. Monitor stickers stuck to his chest and belly. His scar on his chest shone clearly. And his smile lit up his entire face and the room. To be in such discomfort, he still smiled. Every time I look at that picture, I see that I do not have to be my circumstances. Happiness can be found even in a hospital bed. If that little boy can find a reason to keep his chin up and smile like that, then I can be strong for him.

Christopher was discharged at 1:30 pm on Tuesday, October 22nd.

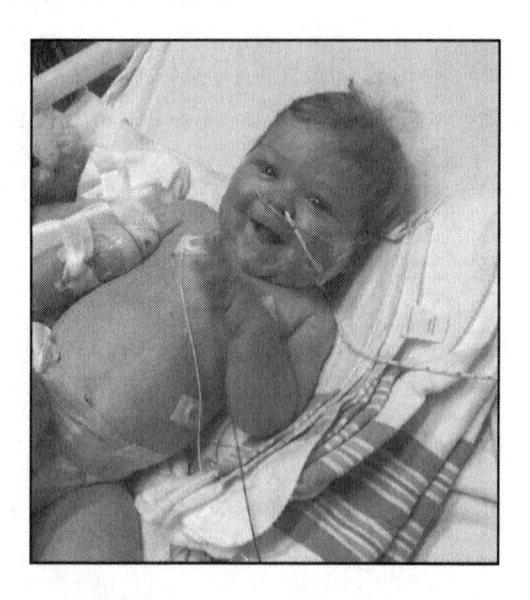

The last picture I took of our little Lionheart.

Thursday, October 24, 2013

Final Post

Several hours after coming home from the hospital in Johnson City on Tuesday, Christopher stopped breathing. We reacted quickly. I called 9-1-1 while Scott tried to revive him. An ambulance got him to our local emergency room. From there a Medjet from Vanderbilt came to pick him up to take him to Nashville. I rode with him in the jet. We arrived at Vanderbilt, and the team in the ICU where Christopher has spent so much time in the past went to work on him. Many of the doctors and nurses had already cared for him in February and July. I was not able to be in the room with him, but doctors gave me updates all along. After the team worked on him for four hours, it was determined that he would not live off of life support. I was able to hold him as his heart rate dropped and he slipped from this world. I keep thinking of the monolog from *Steel Magnolias* when Sally Fields says, "I was there when that beautiful creature drifted into my life, and I was there when he drifted out. It was the most precious moment of my life."

It is the most unnatural feeling to lose a child. It is not the order of things. I will never know why God took Christopher from us at only eight months old, but I find comfort in the words of a friend: "You will either get to raise him here, or you'll get to raise him in heaven. Either way, he'll always be your little boy." This thought does not stop the pain or the tears, but it does mean that it is not ultimately the end.

I've never known of someone so young who touched the lives of so many who never even met him. He has shown people what it's like to take on incredible obstacles head on. He has restored some people's faith in God. He has taught us that even while lying in a hospital bed you can find a reason to smile.

And so this journey has come to an end almost exactly a year after it started. From the moment we found out that Christopher would be born fighting, we have fought for him in every way that we could. It is right that the season is fall. As the leaves are falling leaving the trees to appear bare and lifeless, so it seems from where we sit that Christopher is gone. But he has only gone from this world. He has been taken to a place where he does not hurt anymore. He can run and play and be with loved ones who have gone before him until we get there to see him again. Our baby boy, our little Lionheart will be greatly missed. Christopher, we love you, and we thank God above for the time we had with you.

Losing a child should kill a parent instantly. The pain felt from that loss should be enough to end life. I kept looking down at my chest just below my throat to see the gaping, gnarled, bloody hole that surely must have been there. I felt it. It was like being shot at point blank range in the chest. My soul was mortally wounded. By all other accounts, I was the same. But how could that be? I wanted to die. I wanted to go with my baby boy because there was no way he should go somewhere without me. I felt guilty for him being dead without me with him. No, it wasn't logical. It was severe pain, shock and guilt that made me think those things. Losing a child should kill a parent instantly. But it doesn't. Then what?

You keep breathing. You keep breathing at first because it is an involuntary function. If it wasn't for the human body's design to breathe in and out without conscious thought, I would have just stopped. But God designed us masterfully. So my lungs kept breathing. My heart, though it ached, kept beating. Scott felt the same way. As the father, the leader, the protector he not only felt the severe pain of the loss of our son, he felt like a failure. His expertise in medicine, as keen as it was, was powerless to save our youngest boy. We wanted to comfort each other, but we didn't know how. How could we when we ourselves were torn up and barely able to function?

Our other children. How do we pick up the pieces for them? They've lost a brother. We wanted to stop their pain. So we hurt for our loss of our son and their loss of their brother. How can a body stand this? In the pain, in the confusion, in the helplessness, there was only one answer. We turned to God. Losing a child will kill a parent, maybe not instantly, but the soul will die without the help of the Creator. But I know that the help did not come until I prayed and asked for it. It's that whole "free will" thing. God will come, but you must ask. So I asked—begged really. At first I asked God to take the pain away, and like a snapshot flashing in my mind's eye, He showed me my prayer that I prayed when Christopher was in my womb. "Please let something be wrong with me instead of him." And the prayer I prayed when his Glenn was going badly: "Lord, I'll take his place. I will hurt in his stead." He was showing me that my prayer had been answered. I was hurting and Christopher was not. Plain and simple.

Truth be told, if Christopher could have relayed a message to us from his new heavenly dwelling, he probably would have told us not to cry for him. He is well. No more pain, no more weakness, no more doctors, no more surgery. He is in the eternal presence of God the Father and Jesus Christ. I rejoice in that knowledge! I still cry because I miss him in this mortal life. When I cry for the missed opportunity of raising him and seeing him become a man, I remember the words of our friend Tara: "You'll either raise him here, or you'll raise him in Heaven." So there is hope. Yes, there is still pain and longing, but above all there is hope. Because of the promise of Heaven, there is hope.

EPILOGUE

Christopher Scott Bontrager died on October 23, 2013. I had no reason to know this before he passed, but when a child dies, an autopsy is mandatory. We would have wanted one anyway to find out what happened. Guilt was threatening to consume me.

Sara's birthday is in the middle of November, so that year we took her and a few of her friends to Chuck E. Cheese to celebrate. Scott had received the autopsy report for Christopher two weeks prior to this, and I'm not sure why he chose this time and place to share the results with me. I never asked him why. I figured there was not a good time or place, so he just spilled what he knew.

"The report showed that he became septic secondary to pneumonia. The hospital should have caught it, but they sent him home still very sick." He told me with anger in his voice. Someone had dropped the ball and our little boy paid the price for it with his life.

"The report also showed the beginnings of liver and kidney failure independent of the pneumonia," he continued. "He would have needed a liver or kidney transplant or both before he was Sara's age. He was a sick little boy, love. His life would have been much harder than we imagined." Scott's voice had become more tender. He felt what I do now. There are things worse than death.

I don't know how I held it together during that conversation. It must have been shock. I, of course, fell apart later at this news.

When Scott began medical school, he was studying birth defects. We both knew this would come up. He was down in his basement office studying when I took him a glass of sweet tea and saw on his computer that he was in the middle of studying hypoplastic left heart syndrome. I wrapped my arms around his chest and laid my head on his back trying to comfort him. "This heart defect manifests at 18 days gestation. You probably didn't even know you were pregnant yet before this started happening."

He didn't know it at the time, but I was beating myself up not knowing what I may have done to cause our son's condition. Doctors had reassured us time after time that this was not my fault. It was a genetic disorder that had a terribly minute chance of happening. Scott had always said, "One in a million odds is no consolation to the one."

I don't believe that God did this to our little boy. We live in a fallible world where bad things happen. We were never promised a life void of loss and suffering. It is what we do with the trials in our lives that defines us. I choose love over hate. Hope over bitterness. Positivity over despair. Some days I have a "Christopher day" when the grief overtakes my mood. I could let it consume me, but with the help of Jesus Christ, my Savior, and my Heavenly Father who both love me and I know feel my pain, I make it through.

Made in the USA
Charleston, SC
08 August 2015